My Rory

My Rory

◆

A Personal Journey Through Teenage Anorexia

Alyssa Biederman

with background from her mother,
Janet Biederman

iUniverse, Inc.
New York Lincoln Shanghai

My Rory
A Personal Journey Through Teenage Anorexia

Copyright © 2005 by Alyssa L. Biederman

All rights reserved. No part of this book may be used or reproduced by any means, graphic, electronic, or mechanical, including photocopying, recording, taping or by any information storage retrieval system without the written permission of the publisher except in the case of brief quotations embodied in critical articles and reviews.

iUniverse books may be ordered through booksellers or by contacting:

iUniverse
2021 Pine Lake Road, Suite 100
Lincoln, NE 68512
www.iuniverse.com
1-800-Authors (1-800-288-4677)

Cover illustrated by: Michelle St. John

ISBN: 0-595-34147-0

Printed in the United States of America

I dedicate this book to all those who have suffered from an eating disorder and to their family and friends who have supported them along the way.

Contents

Foreword xi
Preface xiii
About Myself 1
Becoming a Stranger 4
My Darkest Hours 8
Some History 11
  Janet Biederman
Three Meals a Day Keep Barbara Away 16
Counseling 20
  Janet Biederman
Journal Entries Summer 2004 22
The Last Straw 45
  Janet Biederman
More Journal Entries, 2004 49
About Rory 93
The Aftermath 96
Ending Comments 98
  Janet Biederman

Acknowledgments

This book wouldn't be possible without the never-ending support of my family. Their unconditional love and patience were instrumental in my journey toward recovery.

Also, I don't know what I would have done without my best friend, Hayley. She stood by me at my darkest hours and never judged me.

Many thanks to those who cared enough to ask if I was okay and to go out of their way to let me know how much they cared.

To all my friends who were able to make me smile and laugh.

To the many people along the way who helped in my healing process including Barbara, my counselor and Ms. Nosetine.

"We needed to launch a battle; a battle we had to win."

Foreword

by Janet Biederman

From the outside looking in, my daughter appeared to have it all. She was gorgeous, fun to be around, athletic, smart and incredibly fit. Most important, she projected an incredible kindness to others masking her confused inner mind. Why would someone so blessed be so insecure about her appearance-the outer shell that looked so perfect to others? I asked that question to myself over and over again.

I don't even know where to begin to explain the depth of pain experienced while working through the eating disorder that enveloped my daughter. We were and are so very close. As a parent, I wanted to blame myself. If only I could take back the times I commented on the frequent trips to Wendy's upon getting her driver's license, perhaps this never would have happened. Now, a trip to Wendy's brings only heartache. Instead of the standard junior bacon cheeseburger and fries, chili is substituted as the only meal of the day. Just thinking of the past year brings me to tears.

I'll never forget the weekend of my 39th birthday in February 2004. It marked the beginning of a painful and slow journey toward recovery. It was the weekend that finally convinced my husband and I it was time to reach out to someone from the outside. Our perfect little family had a very serious problem-one too big to deal with alone. All of *the signs were there, but for some reason it took overhearing a conversation with her boyfriend that gave us the final signal that said "GET HELP NOW!" We needed to launch a battle; a battle we had to win.*

My husband and I spent the weekend talking, crying, praying and searching for answers. Finally, at midnight on Sunday as my husband and I rummaged through our health care information, we came across a telephone number for a crisis hotline referral program. The next day, I called the psychologist to whom we were referred and prepared myself for the conversation I would have with Alyssa after school. As expected, she was in complete denial. But deep down, I know she knew she needed help. She agreed to go to the appointment. Please, God, let this be the answer...

"We share a common bond. We are all alike."

Preface

You're right. I don't know you. I have not lived your life and you have certainly not lived mine. I do, however, know your type. You wake up every morning and look in the mirror critiquing your body from all angles as you walk toward the scale. The number determines more than just your mood. It sets your plan, your goal for the day. You base your day around that number. You grab an apple for breakfast. At night you carefully measure a cup of dry cereal and place it in a brown paper bag along with some carrots for lunch the next day.

At school you walk down the halls and feel like people are staring at the excess fabric on your once tight jeans. But that can't be-you know you are still fat and feel like you need to push harder to lose weight. At lunch, your table mates joke about your strangely packed lunches. Although their comments hurt, you brush it off hiding the pain and secret life inside.

Throughout the day you obsessively recount the number of consumed calories to make sure you don't go over your set "limit." You sit in class debating about which meal would be a better choice for dinner. If a friend asks you last minute to go out to eat, an intense rush of anxiety fills your mind. What will you eat? How can you figure out the calories of your meal if you don't know what ingredients went into making it? When will you have more time to exercise?

You exercise repetitively, usually in secret, hoping to burn off more calories than you ate. You count every step. Sitting still is unacceptable.

Although you are hungry, you are afraid to eat. You are afraid that once you start eating, you may have no control…and you crave control. Unless your meal is preplanned, eating ends in guilt and you think about flushing your problems down the toilet. You might do it, or you will exercise twice as much as normal and starve yourself the next couple days. Either way, you are haunted by your disgusting so-called binge for days.

Finally once friends and family start noticing your new habits, everything changes. You feel trapped. They force you to eat a "normal" meal, known to you as poison. They follow you when you walk into the bathroom and try to restrict your exercise routines. As far as you're concerned, they add to the chaos inside your mind-that little voice that never fades, pushing you farther and farther away.

How do I know about the twists and turns that scatter in your brain and the thoughts that fill your mind every second of the day? I know because I have walked in your shoes.

◆ ◆ ◆

Not all sufferers of an eating disorder end up hospitalized or lose such a tremendous amount of weight their bodies resemble skeletal replicas. Anorexia as well as other eating disorders is a very misunderstood and dangerous disorder of both the mind and body. Just because my story does not include the physical extremities to the extent of hospitalization or elapsed length does not make my experience any less real. The suffering I felt was no different from anyone else. The confusion in our minds simply cannot be explained. We share a common bond. We are all alike.

Once you work past denial, you ask yourself why me? Why was I put through this fight between my body and mind? Why did nearly a year of my life have to take so much from me? And why was I put through months of hell and depression that to this day has not fully disappeared? There has to be a reason.

As the clouds began to move away and the sun started to shine I think I may have figured it out. I grew up hearing "everything happens for a reason." As much as I have hated every moment of my suffering, I now know my answer to "why me?" And that is where this book comes into play. I want to help others realize they are not alone.

When I actually realized I was about to share my feelings and personal life with strangers, I became hesitant. I was afraid of what others would say or think. I was afraid of being labeled or judged for the rest of my life now that the painful truth would be out. If I learned one thing throughout high school (besides whom your true friends are) it is "don't explain yourself; your friends don't need it and the others won't believe it." Keeping that quote in mind, I decided to follow through in publishing my story. I no longer feel the need to explain my choices with food, or feel ashamed. I do, however, believe I have a responsibility to let others know this disorder can be treated and they are not alone. I am doing better, but I would be lying if I said I was completely healed because I am not. In many ways the thoughts and confusion of this disorder are still there and I have a feeling that they always will be in some form. I can feel it deep inside my heart. Some days the struggle is more prominent than others and I can almost feel it pushing trying to make me crack. Most days I barely notice it at all, but I know it is there. I feel it both emotionally and physically. I wish I could just count to ten and make a wish that my heart would magically be healed, but I can't. The past year of memories will forever be cemented in my mind.

I believe no one can understand the true feelings and fears of a person suffering from an eating disorder unless they themselves have suffered. I know that getting well is simply not a matter of choice. I wouldn't wish this disorder on my worst enemy. I figure that if I can help just one person in any way, then I have succeeded. Perhaps you are not the person suffering from an eating disorder, but rather a family member or friend struggling to find answers and help the person you love. I share my story for you.

"They say life doesn't change overnight, but I know it can."

About Myself

Relationships throughout the past few years have defined my growth and stability in life. My parents, brother and I have always shared a unique bond. Our level of comfort talking openly about topics has surprised and shocked many. My mom and I share a friendship that many teenage girls would envy, despite our disagreements and conflicting views, I am the spitting image of my mom and proud to admit it.

I come from what most would call "The All-American Family." My mom is without a doubt one of my best friends. I share everything with her. Don't get me wrong, we do have our arguments but I believe the reason we argue is because we are so much alike. My dad has worked hard to provide my brother and I with everything we could ask for and he has always put our family first. My brother, Tyler, is almost four years younger than I am, but is very protective. Our family is close in ways that most can only imagine. My mom and dad represent the relationship I dream of having one day. They met during 8th grade at the bus stop. Throughout all the years, they still are hopelessly in love.

Hayley, has been and will always be more than a best friend and confidant, for she is considered a part of my family. Connected head to foot through heartache, disloyal friends and laughter, she stood by me when I was ready to walk away from myself.

Rory, my boyfriend for nearly two years played a very important role in my life. Although we are no longer together, he taught me one of the most important lessons that will forever remain in my heart. I learned how to love unconditionally with my whole heart and how amazing it feels to be loved.

Although I am uncomfortable talking about my personal achievements, I realize the importance of sharing some history. Like many suffering from eating disorders, I led what was considered the ideal life. I was raised in the affluent community of Perrysburg, Ohio and traveled frequently with my family. I am an honor roll student and two-year member of our school newspaper staff. As a four-year varsity letter winner in girls' tennis, I won the league championship in doubles and qualified for districts in 2003 and 2004. I was also a cheerleader my freshman year and now a member of an all-star competitive cheerleading squad. Volunteering for various organizations such as Hospice and working a part-time job for over a year added to my busy schedule. With so much in my life to be thankful for, the big question is, "how did I fall prey to anorexia?"

I don't think I will ever really have the answer to that question. They say life doesn't change overnight, but I know it can. I am unable to blame one event or series of events for leading me down the lonely path of an eating disorder. Society has this absurd image of the perfect woman and it wasn't me. I recall looking in the mirror one evening feeling uncomfortable with the image I saw staring back. I felt so alone. Tears starting falling down my face. At first, they dropped one by one, but soon they began pouring out like a waterfall. I couldn't stop crying. That evening marked the first day of my new life as an anorexic. At first, I just wanted to lose a couple pounds, but then after I accomplished my goal, losing weight became an addiction.

"I became unlovable to the family who showed me more love than I could ever return, despite the way I treated them."

Becoming a Stranger

Before I new it, my obsession with becoming thinner was out of control. Unable to understand my own confused state of mind, I shut out those I loved and cared about. Sadly, this resulted in the breakup of Rory and I. I lost more than a boyfriend; I lost a friend.

My psychologist, Barbara, suggested I keep a journal to record my innermost thoughts and emotions. I had never really written in a diary or journal before, but I found it much easier to express my feelings in writing than express them verbally. My journal became an emotional outlet which I affectionately referred to as "My Rory."

◆　◆　◆

Around the house, I was not the same energetic, loving daughter and sister I used to be. I picked arguments, bickered and complained all the time. I refused to eat with the family, began to hate home-cooked meals and learned to make up excuses for everything. I found myself constantly picking my family apart with ridicule. I became unlovable to the family who showed me more love than I could ever return, despite the way I treated them.

Along with my family, Hayley became frustrated, irritable and impatient with my persistent lack of eating and exercise habits. Until that year, I never believed anything could shake our friendship. I certainly pushed the limits. I became annoyed with her constant concern while she became angry with my blindness to the illness that was taking over my life.

I am lucky that my eating disorder did not permanently change or ruin the relationships with my family and friends. However, it did push away someone I loved deeply. Sometimes, no matter how hard you pray, you can't go back and change the past and to this day, it still haunts me. To some extent, I believe the future is in your own hands. At the age of 17, ending my junior year I played catch and dropped that ball filled with love and friendship. It shattered while the pieces blew away. I spent months trying to pick up all the pieces, but it is impossible. Some pieces have been carried out of my reach.

At the time I knew that I was treating Rory unfairly. I recognized my shortness, nagging, sarcasm, irritation and utter rudeness and disrespect. However, I simply did not care. Months of despair and repetition sent us our separate ways. The worst part is that the sole conflict was based on something controllable although at times it did not appear the case. Whether we would still be sharing a remarkable relationship or would have been together only a month or so longer, I will never know. But that is the beauty in it. There are many things you will not ever know which makes life all the more interesting and anticipating. You are given the accessibility to dream. Your dreams have no limitations, but life on the other hand does.

♦   ♦   ♦

"Live life with no regrets." In all honesty, I don't believe an individual can succeed at such a goal. We all aim to pursue this goal, but in reality is it possible? I personally, being brought up by an optimistic mother, have strived for perfection in all my actions and overall, I have been fairly successful. We often look back on conversations wishing we had spoken our deepest feelings or expressed with actions how we truly feel about the people that surround us. After my breakup with Rory, I did just that. I laid my emotions on the line and I have no regrets. He knows exactly how I feel about him and the conflicts during the last few months of our relationship. With that being said, my final regret is my struggle during my junior year. Unfortunately that struggle is not one I can take back. I have however learned to accept my junior year and am now using my weakness in turn as a strength. I regret the way I treated Rory during our last few months not only because I hurt someone I cared about but because I lost someone that I probably otherwise would not have. On the contrary I still believe everything happens for a reason and with that being said, I have the courage to move on…

♦   ♦   ♦

June 3, 2004-About a week ago I was babysitting for two little girls around the ages of three and five. While playing outside in the front yard and watching them run and fall in the grass, I remembered being that young when the fall was just a little stumble to the ground considering your top half was only two or three feet from your toes. As I observed,

I felt that although I am nearly three and a half feet taller, I feel closer to the ground than ever. Almost as if I could crash right into it.

◆ ◆ ◆

My eating disorder singled me out from my family and friends. The fights in my mind, and emotional strain could not be understood by others no matter how hard they tried. Writing out my thoughts to read to myself became the only way I could express my feelings and share my story. These entries became my voice. In a way, I wish I had started writing in my journal months before during the peak of my eating disorder. In other ways, I am glad I did not. I am afraid of what I would look back upon. I remember everything, every single detail from that year, yet reading what I wrote those dark days would only haunt me more.

"It was not until I started living that I realized I was dead."

My Darkest Hours

Contrary to my parents and close friends who view my darkest point taking place in the midst of recovery, I felt trapped prior to when they realized. On the outside no one noticed. I had a talent-a talent of hiding my anxiety, depression, frustration, pain and lack of self-worth and confidence. I laughed it off, making sarcastic comments and cracking jokes aiming to yield the truth. While playing off perfection in every aspect, I felt as though I was about to fall at any moment. In fact, sometimes I felt I did such a good job at acting, I should try out for the next drama play in school. Once my family and Hayley became aware and involved, everything changed. My life fell into a downward spiral. I was no longer able to hide, and I hated accepting that. Accepting my inability to hide what I once hid so well was vital to recovery. It was not until then I began to understand how alone I felt. I tried to hide my obsession by lying to my psychologist Barbara and my family. Sometimes I got away with the lies. Other times they saw through them. It was not until I started actually living that I realized I was dead.

What I Don't Want

*I don't want to be that girl
that swears off fatty meats
that exercises after everything she eats
I don't want to be that girl
who fears a piece of cake
and throws up after every meal she makes
I don't want to be that girl
who looks into the mirror
and cannot help but shed a tiny tear
I don't want to be that girl
you see on the street
hiding beneath baggy clothes from head to feet
I don't want to be that girl who measures what she eats
who steps on a scale afraid of defeat
I don't want to be that girl
that records calories in a book
figuring every bite she last took
I don't want to be that girl
who loses too much weight
whose parents fear her future fate
I don't want to be that girl
Who begins to fade
due to the poor choices she made
I don't want to be that girl
who slowly starts to die*

as friends let out a last plea and goodbye
I don't want to be that girl
on the covers of magazines
What I really want is ME; a healthy, well-developed teen.
-Alyssa-

"The once glowing beauty was becoming a frail, weak child."

Some History...

Janet Biederman

In May of 2003, I took Alyssa to the doctor for an upper respiratory infection. Her weight was 118 pounds I vividly remember the nurse saying to her "wow you are so thin." Alyssa then commented to me that it was the most she had ever weighed and couldn't believe it. I reminded her she was thinner than the average sixteen year old at five feet five inches tall and that I would gladly trade her places.

♦ ♦ ♦

In the fall of 2003, Alyssa's boyfriend of one and a half years headed off to college. We knew this would be difficult for her, but they seemed to have figured out how they could continue to see each other and make their relationship work. Looking back, I am sure there was some thought in her mind that she would now be competing against 10,000 girls on a college campus instead of the 600 in high school. It is not that her boyfriend wasn't good to her or didn't make her feel special. I know he did. But he also never hesitated to point out someone that was on the heavier side or joke around about someone eating more than they should.

Tennis season had also begun in the fall and Alyssa started making subtle changes to her diet. She passed up the daily Wendy's for her own packed lunches. At first, I thought she was simply making healthier choices since I had always harassed her about the daily burgers and fries. I had no idea she was trying to lose weight Then, toward the end of the tennis season, she had a muscle injury requiring a doctor's visit. She approached the scale. She now weighed 112 pounds. A six pound difference in five months. Considering it was the peak of the tennis season, her weight loss did not seem abnormal.

◆   ◆   ◆

Shortly thereafter I was becoming keenly aware of the odd behavior and obsession Alyssa began to have with working out. I also noticed she was wearing layers of clothing attempting to hide the weight loss. In looking through her closet I noticed her size five jeans were pushed to the corner and her size threes were becoming noticeably loose. It's a phase I told myself after approaching her about my concerns and getting reassurance that everything was "under control."

In November, Alyssa and I made a trip to the gynecologist. Her periods were becoming unpredictable. At the time, I did not associate the problems she was having with her weight loss. Despite the fact Alyssa weighed in at only 108 pounds, there was never any mention or concern about her weight. Therefore, it never occurred to me to point it out. Her appointment went well otherwise and she was cleared to start birth control pills. Ironically, she needed to have a period before she could begin taking the pill. More than two weeks past her "due date" she finally started. This period was extremely light and most likely would have been her last for a long time had she not started birth control pills to force a period as her weight loss and food deprivation continued.

◆ ◆ ◆

While the rest of our family ate dinner together, Alyssa always found an excuse not to join us. When she did eat, she would limit herself to watermelon, Kashi cereal, rice cakes, celery and carrots. These were foods she never would have touched before. She was obsessed with the fiber content of food as well. She stopped eating the lunch at school and began packing. Her packed lunches would consist of carrots and celery. Adding an apple or banana made it a fat day in her mind. A mere mention of concern about her lack of food would result in an argument. "I AM EATING or I JUST ATE A PEANUT BUTTER SANDWICH, CRACKERS AND SOME CHEESE." Her responses were so quick, that we believed her in the beginning. It wasn't until later we learned how to catch her in the little white lies.

◆ ◆ ◆

Reality was setting in and we were finally able to put the pieces of the puzzle together. We began to analyze the series of events leading up to this point-all the signs were there, we just couldn't see them clearly. The stunning daughter and sister we all knew and loved was becoming someone we barely recognized. Her outgoing demeanor became introverted. It was becoming increasingly obvious that this was no longer a phase. Losing weight was becoming a dangerous obsession.

Not a day went by when Alyssa wasn't complaining about the cold. She froze all the time. I began to think she had a circulatory problem and feared other conditions not realizing at first this was all related to her lack of nutrition, weight, etc. She would get dizzy and look pale. The once glowing beauty, was becoming a frail weak child.

She lacked the proper nutrition and minerals to even think rationally. She got mad easily. If she walked into the kitchen while someone else was eating she would go nuts. She couldn't stand to hear the sound of food being chewed. It would send her in a rage. Her temperament was out of control for one reason. She was starving. Foods she once loved and asked for were now considered taboo. When she did allow herself to eat, it resulted in a guilt trip. She considered any meal a binge. We silently celebrated with each bite she took.

I used to look forward to when she would come home from school and sit at the kitchen counter to share her day with me. Some of our best conversations took place at the counter. She shared everything with me, but lately this routine had changed. She now retreated to her room where within moments I would start to hear the constant thumping from the ceiling indicating her exercise regimen had begun. Our once peaceful conversations resulted in arguments over exercising.

Alyssa's bones were starting to protrude from her neckline yet she was constantly commenting about being overweight. She walked into the bathroom frequently hopping on the scale. She became dangerously dependent of this evil machine. I had no choice. I snuck it out of the house, placed it in my husband's car and asked him to get rid of it for good. I couldn't risk putting it in the trash as I knew she would rummage through it until it was found. Other habits consisted of glancing in the mirror at every opportunity and constantly picking at her skin trying to find the fat that did not exist. What was going on inside her mind? Why couldn't she see what we did?

◆ ◆ ◆

Alyssa often talked about how much she was beginning to hate school. It wasn't school she hated. It was the comments and snickers from other students about what she did or didn't eat at lunch that she hated. This created a fearful environment of anxiety. She even felt hurt for the other girls being talked about that she knew were struggling with weight issues. Didn't they realize how much their comments hurt? I could see the pain in Alyssa's eyes each day. It was all I could do to keep from calling these girls and scream. In fact, why didn't anyone besides her best friend, Hayley, care enough to share their concern? They could all talk and laugh about it, but they refused to reach out and help. Hayley's genuine love and concern for Alyssa was comforting.

Throughout this whole ordeal, I often wondered why other people weren't approaching us with concern. Are we making more of an issue of this than we should?

In time there were a couple school staff members and friends who did approach Alyssa. Sadly, they never approached us. They did, however, express their concern later and only when I brought the subject up. It was then I learned how much they really did care and had great concern for her, but were not sure how to approach the subject. Why I wondered? That validation would have made it so much easier for us to seek outside help sooner without the fear we would be passed off as worrying too much. Why weren't the school guidance counselors trained to recognize and seek out students who obviously needed support? Alyssa was not the only student struggling with an eating disorder. Thankfully, we sought the help we needed on our own. I worry so much for others who are not as lucky to have a family with the foresight to understand the seriousness of this disease.

"Watching my mom cry because of her worries, hurt almost more than the effects of the illness itself."

Three Meals a Day Keep Barbara Away

I vividly recall the first time Barbara actually got firm about my weight. Throughout my sessions with her, she never told me to eat more food or gain weight. She focused on my feelings. My last visit with her before spring break, she pulled my mom and I into a small office after my session with her was over. She spoke firmly and directly at me expressing her concern that my weight loss was getting dangerous. She said I looked unhealthy, entirely too skinny and had lost color in my skin. She threatened that if I did not gain a few pounds by the time I returned to her in three weeks, she would have to do something else as my condition was very serious. I was in shock. Throughout the first two months with Barbara she had never expressed her concern like this and it scared the hell out of me.

Upon my return three weeks later, I had put on a couple pounds and my mom shared with Barbara that things appeared to be improving. I thought after the next few visits I had proved I was on the right track, but Barbara still saw something different. I can distinctly remember walking in and her criticizing my still skinny stature. She felt that I had lost weight again and I was covering up trying to play off a new "improved lifestyle." At that point she took me into another room and had me step on a scale. That was the first time she had made me do that, I wasn't even aware that she had a scale in her office. She was not happy.

In early spring I was put on Paxil for anticipatory anxiety. Anxiety is a common problem for those suffering from eating disorders. The medication helped ease my preoccupation with food. As both my doctor and psychologist hoped, it also contributed to quicker weight gain.

I think the hardest visits with my psychologist, were the visits when my mom was in the room with me. My mom would voice her concerns about my weight loss and our relationship slipping. Watching my mom cry because of her worries, hurt almost more than the effects of the illness itself.

◆ ◆ ◆

I went from sharing the truth about everything from relationships with family, friends, my boyfriend and classmates to flat out lies. I lied about what I ate for lunch. I denied that I was irritable and picked arguments with my boyfriend. Then there was Barbara. The one reason I began to become fed up with her guidance and theories was because she was on to me and my deceit. I couldn't lie to her anymore.

Some conclusions she came to were what I considered out of whack, but for the most part, she was completely right. In all honesty, she did help. At the time, I would not have admitted it for a minute, but looking back, she made a difference. She did this simply by listening. During our sessions, all I wanted to do was break down. Occasionally I did, but for the most part I fought to keep everything inside. Toward our last few sessions, I closed up. I no longer wanted to share my life with her. I did not find comfort in sharing my daily concerns and struggles. I felt like a failure. In the meantime, she tried to pry out my feelings. I tried to stand up for myself and denied everything she assumed I was doing or not doing. Sadly, she was right about most everything.

I stopped my appointments with her in May. Barbara helped shed light on my problems. After she started me on the right path, I knew no one else could push me farther along, but myself. I debated continuing my sessions, but I decided that only I could choose to get better. I held the power. No one could help me improve from that point if I did not want to.

◆   ◆   ◆

I tried to eat at a set time every day. When I came home from school, I was so hungry, I couldn't wait to eat. I craved my bowl of cereal throughout classes. I wandered around the house aimlessly, creating small projects in an attempt to distract my mind from food. I gave in several times and ate my dinner as early as four o'clock. Although, I never felt like doing anything, I tried to keep busy. I figured if I had something to do it would keep me from eating. On days I met with Barbara, I thought of it as an hour I would be away from food. However, if the appointment lapsed into my eating schedule, I freaked. When would I eat?

Sunday mornings and afternoons became my lowest calorie day of the week. I worked at Bob Evans from 10:00 a.m. until 4:30 p.m. I chose not to eat on break, yet told my parents I ordered a grilled cheese sandwich so I could get away with a half peanut butter sandwich for dinner. I hated my job at Bob Evans. The only positive side to this job besides the money was the six and a half hours I could easily get away with not eating.

I recorded my calorie intake daily in my school assignment notebook. I used this to keep track of my success. If I did well by keeping calories and grams of fat low for the week, I would allow myself a treat on the weekend. This notebook became the agenda of my life.

"I was beginning to wonder how I could help someone who refused to acknowledge she had a problem."

Counseling...

Janet Biederman

We began meeting with Barbara, a psychologist in February. Most of the sessions focused very little on the weight loss itself. In April 2004, Alyssa's psychologist finally did what I hoping she'd do. After meeting with Alyssa, I was called into the room and for the first time Barbara made a threat that was absolutely necessary. "You will gain a few pounds in three weeks or we will be looking into more desperate measures of treatment. Your situation is quite serious." No one had to ask what she meant. It had become apparent to me that a treatment center may very well be our next step if immediate changes were not made. In many ways, I was relieved by Barbara's comments. We were also asked to pay a visit to her family doctor for blood work to check her electrolytes, etc. It was also suggested (for the 3rd time) that we consider medication such as Paxil to help with the anticipatory anxiety Alyssa dealt with related to food.

We did everything we were asked to do, but Alyssa "faked" her way into allowing Barbara and I to think she had gained weight on her next visit. By layering clothes, tanning, and putting on a smile, she walked into her next appointment bragging of the couple pounds she had supposedly gained and how she felt she was on the right track. In *fact her demeanor was so much better, she was taken off the "urgent" watch and was given her next appointment-6 weeks out. Unbelievable, I thought. Alyssa seemed to be doing well in my eyes too, until...*

The middle of May when Alyssa went to her high school sports physical and she told me with a scary sense of excitement she weighed in at 102 pounds. I told her I was calling Barbara for an earlier appointment. She proceeded to tell me she would not go back to her for an appointment-ever. I suspect because Barbara finally came out with the truth and that truth hurt. I was beginning to wonder how I could help someone who refused to acknowledge she had a problem.

"When the people I love and trust began creating images I couldn't see, I struggled even more."

Journal Entries
Summer 2004

So mom wasn't exactly pleased today when she found out that I weighed 102 pounds at my physical. All I could do was remind her that it is slowly getting better. I've gotten used to talking openly about my issues with eating. In the beginning I didn't want people knowing that I was seeing a special counselor or that I was put on Paxil for anxiety. Unfortunately, I found out the hard way that when you lose 15 pounds in a couple of months, people start to figure things out for themselves and they talk, especially behind your back. Throughout everything in the last few months, realizing people really do care has made a huge difference in my recovery. Some people went out of their way a lot more than others. I am thankful for Hayley taking me out of class to voice her concerns to the school counselor and constantly watching out for me, Dan calling out of the blue to express how much he cares and bringing me a Mr. Freeze Peanut Butter Cup Sundae to assure me it was ok to eat, Teresa dropping off a supportive card and everyone else that in some way has made a subtle comment or gesture to show they care. Unfortunately, not everyone contributed in such a positive manner. A comic was made recently by a friend titled "Prom in a Nutshell."

I wasn't supposed to see it, however, I did. In the corner of the picture was a stick figure drawn with an arrow saying, "Alyssa in the bathroom puking because she's bulimic." And then there was a time someone started rambling off comments at lunch to someone loud enough for the whole table to hear. These included "At least I'm not a bitch, at least my pants fit me and I'm not anorexic." Wow and to hear from her the next day that those were about me. Oh and believe me there's plenty more where that came from…but hey on the bright side at least some people had the courage to ask me to my face if I was anorexic. I don't think I could even count how many people mentioned something to Hayley if not to me.

The comments that were made by my table mates during lunch became repetitive and hurtful. It seemed like every day someone different would comment on my choice of packed lunch or my skinny arms and slightly baggy pants. They were my friends, and still are. Looking back now I know why their choice of words stuck with me for months to come. It wasn't because I cared what they thought of me, it was simply because their comments were reality, a reality that I wasn't ready to face.

Friends weren't the only ones that noticed the weight I lost. The assistant principal, who was also my 8th grade cheerleading coach, asked me how much weight I lost. I acted clueless to brush it off, but she insisted that I had lost weight recently. A matter of fact, two months into my senior year, she ran into my mother at my brother's football game leading to an in depth conversation concerning my situation the year before. She explained to my mother that she wanted to pick up the phone several times over the course of the year in fear of the weight I lost, and regrets the fact that she never did. (Luckily, my parents picked up on the symptoms.) She indicated that some staff members were aware of my situation and were secretly looking out for me. The school was worried about what was tearing me apart, and I was oblivious. My mom expressed her concern about what was going on during lunch and my mom was told that if I ever faced uncomfortable situations during lunch again, I had permission to leave and sit either in her office or a teacher's with no questions asked in order to prevent a possible relapse.

Even one of the employees of a local tanning salon mentioned something to me one evening. (I used tanning to hide the lack of color in my skin tone) She told me I looked like I had lost a lot of weight. Once again, without wanting to face it, I explained I was wearing a pair of jeans which were a size or two big. I remember walking into the tanning booth afterwards as tears started pouring down my cheeks. When someone I barely knew began making comments to me about my weight I became even more confused. Whom could I trust? Why would a stranger tell me something if it wasn't somewhat true? Why couldn't I see things the way they did? It was a battle then and still is today. I have always had difficulty trusting people. To me, trust is one of the most powerful virtues one can possess. When the people I love and trust began creating images I couldn't see, I struggled even more.

◆ ◆ ◆

I just started reading a book that my mom bought for me today. It's about a girl's struggle with an eating disorder. The saddest thing is I feel like I am reading about my own life. Her emotions and thoughts are a lot like mine.

♦ ♦ ♦

    I went to visit Brett for the weekend. He is a boy I met during spring break in April on a cruise in the Caribbean. He came to visit me a couple weeks ago. When he asked me to visit and go with him to a concert, I knew it would be good for me to get away. I got to meet a lot of his friends and for the first time in a while, I allowed myself to have fun. Then, the next morning Brett's mom made breakfast for us before I left. As she got out the ingredients, I noticed that the milk she used to make the french toast was whole, full fat milk. For a split second I felt a knot in my stomach and a rush of anxiety. I even noticed myself trying to count up the calories repeatedly in my head. Trying my best to focus on something else, I quickly finished my meal.

♦ ♦ ♦

    I did something horrible. The last few days at random times I have completely binged on food. I feel like I have no control over what I put in my mouth. This morning I stuffed my face with food I did not need. Afterwards, as if it were ritual I walked into the bathroom and flushed my "problems" away. I felt relieved yet disgusted. I have only done this once before and I know I will never do it again. After that, still feeling guilty, I decided to go for a run to burn off the calories I may not have thrown up.

♦ ♦ ♦

    Last week I was thinking about how I just want to get away for a while to be alone. I had a week in the Caribbean in mind, not a treatment center. My parents looked into treatment centers for eating disor-

ders to take my recovery a step further. Apparently there is one only 20 minutes away. Who would have known!? We had a discussion this afternoon about the possibility of me becoming a patient there. I would be put on a waiting list after completing a detailed questionnaire. Once accepted, I would have 24 hour inpatient care from one to six weeks. They also have an outpatient program I may be eligible for. Their program attracts patients from around the country. I told my parents I believed it wasn't necessary and tried to buy myself some time. They questioned my confidence but I think I'm safe from going there…at least for now. As much of a disappointment summer has been so far, spending the rest of it in a building while doctors and counselors observe my every move doesn't exactly sound like a vacation.

◆ ◆ ◆

Once again I completely binged on food tonight. I couldn't control it and I hated that feeling. What followed afterwards was another mistake. Yes, I felt much better but I really never want to do that again. God, please watch over me and give me the strength to never give into my weakness. I don't want to purge again. I don't want to get worse, more than anything I want to get better.

◆ ◆ ◆

Out of curiosity my mom and I decided to drive by the treatment center before going to the mall. It was a bit out of the way, but for some reason I was curious to see what it was like. The building looked just like a small hospital and only two other cars were in the parking lot. My mom and I tried to go in to see if they had any pamphlets, however all the lights were off and the doors were locked because it was the weekend.

Walking back to the car, I felt weak glancing back at the building and windows on the second floor. It felt almost as though the patients were peering out at me. By just driving by, I know that I never want to end up there. As we pulled away, I could sense the fear in my mom's eyes afraid that I could be one of those patients.

◆ ◆ ◆

Well the truth came out...doesn't it always. My friends were over and we were having a good time. I walked into the bathroom with Hayley to share some quick gossip. She quickly turned the conversation around and asked me the same question she had asked me earlier in the day and several times before "Alyssa, have you ever made yourself vomit?" This time, I told the truth. When she found out the truth, her reaction was more dramatic than I expected. She was disappointed that I had not only harmed my body but the fact that I lied to my best friend. At that moment, Christina walked in and heard the secret I had been trying to keep. We hugged and cried and they made me promise I would never do it again. When we exited the bathroom, the two guys that were still over were more confused than ever. They had suspected that I had been dealing with eating issues and now knew the truth. When even your guy friends are showing affection and telling you that you need to gain weight, you start to believe that maybe there is a problem. For that I am thankful, yet frustrated too.

◆ ◆ ◆

My mom knows about the recent purges now too. I came right out and confessed. I could see in her eyes how hurt and disappointed she was. Because I had lied to both my family and best friend before it's hard to convince them that it won't happen again. There is now a new rule in our house. Both the bathroom door and my bedroom door must be open a crack whenever I am in the rooms. I feel like I'm being watched like on those hidden camera shows. It is almost as if they are just waiting for the moment I grow weak and fail. I am beginning to feel like when I'm around my family and friends I have to eat just to please them, not myself.

Today my parents also set a new rule that they say is to be seriously enforced. I have to eat one full-course meal in front of them daily. They have the final decision over what is considered a healthy, balanced meal(meaning no special health or diet foods). They are concerned and worried about what will happen when I leave for college next year. They are afraid of me being gone and relapsing because I won't have someone watching over my eating habits. That is why they have started to get frustrated and are stressing the importance of getting the situation under control completely before I leave.

Well, as if telling me the new rules in our house weren't enough, my parents presented me with a written list today of all the rules which I must follow and agree to. These rules included, but were not limited to:

1. <u>Eating three meals a day, including a healthy snack in between</u>.

2. <u>No exercising every day or in my room</u>. After every bite I consumed all I could think about was how I was going to burn the calories. I did it privately in my room but my parents could hear the hustle above them as they sat in the family room or computer room. I did crunches, leg lifts, ran in place and anything else I read in a magazine that would tone your body. I became

obsessed making sure I burned more calories than I ate. I looked up online how many calories were burned during different activities. I even would think about it while I walked up the steps to school. Everything I did was taken into consideration. If I had to walk an extra few steps, I would be closer to achieving my goal.

3. <u>Showing them everything I eat and eating it in front of them</u>. This was a big one. When I made a sandwich, I had to show it to either my mom or dad. That was the only way they could be sure it contained "enough" peanut butter or meat. If it wasn't up to their standards, they added more. If my parents weren't home, they put Hayley in charge of watching my meals. I felt like I had to base my eating schedule around their time because they never believed me if I told them I already ate, whether it was the truth or not.

4. <u>Not being allowed to be home alone for more than a few minutes</u>. After my parents found out that I had induced vomiting, they watched my every move. If I got up at a restaurant to go to the bathroom, my mom walked in seconds after. If they left me alone, they feared I would only throw up again. If they wanted to go somewhere, they made sure I would be with Hayley or my brother, Tyler. At 17 years of age, I felt like a seven-year-old with a babysitter.

5. <u>Keep the bathroom door open while I shower.</u> Once again, they felt that if the door was open, I wouldn't throw up and they were right. When I got out of the shower, I would actually find my mom sitting right outside of the bathroom. If I accidently forgot and shut the door, she would immediately open it. If I

went to the restroom and she heard the toilet flush she would rush up the steps and ask the question that I heard day after day, "You didn't just do something stupid did you?" On several occasions while using the restroom, I requested the privacy of the door being closed. On these occasions I would have to talk to her the whole time.

6. <u>Keep my bedroom door open a crack during the day</u>. This rule was enforced to restrict my private exercise routine and eliminate the possibility of me purging in my bedroom.

7. <u>No listening to music while in the bathroom</u>. I love music. You name it, I like it, besides jazz that is. I have a shower radio and several times I would bring in a cd player to listen to while I took a long shower or hot bath.. This became no longer an option. It was looked at by them as a way for me to drown out the sounds of gagging.

8. <u>Eating what my mom prepares for dinner with the family</u>. For several months while my mom prepared a wonderful meal for the family, I fixed myself some vegetables or a bowl of cereal skipping the milk. I never ate the dinner that was served. My parents were frustrated and my brother confused. I couldn't even stand to sit with them while they ate the meal that was considered "off limits" to me. Watching them eat disgusted me and made me crave food even more.

◆ ◆ ◆

I just walked into the bathroom and noticed that the scale was gone. I am determined to find where my mom hid it. Not knowing my current weight throughout the day creates panic and anxiety. If I can't weigh myself every day I may gain too much weight without realizing it and I can't let that happen.

◆ ◆ ◆

Walking into the bathroom and not being able to weigh myself has been stressful and it has only been one day. Apparently, my dad took the scale out of the house and it will remain at his office in Detroit, Michigan. I'm scared that I'm getting bigger and not even realizing it.

I don't know what I would call my relationship with the scale. Whether it was considered an obsession or habit, it definitely consumed my life. Perhaps it was a mixture of both. Before my eating disorder began, I cannot recall regularly checking my weight. In fact, when I was younger I don't believe I had a close guess as to my approximate weight. During my eating disorder, I don't think more than a couple of hours went by without checking my weight. Every time I walked into the bathroom to brush my teeth, shower, or clean, I stepped on the scale. It got to the point that I never even thought about it, but it became a ritual. The first thing I would do in the morning was check my weight. It was my favorite time of day because my weight was always the lowest first thing in the morning. The number on the scale determined my mood for the day. The lower the number, the better I felt.

Looking back, I think their decision to get rid of the scale was my first big step to recovery. I slowly learned to not feel dependent on a number and realized that I was more than the hands on a dial. I know if I was able to continue to weigh myself daily, I would not have had the strength to improve.

◆ ◆ ◆

Tonight at Hayley's I was bored and pulled out her yearbook from the table next to her bed. Several sheets of notebook paper were crammed inside, but one specifically caught my eye. It was a list titled "What makes me happy." Among them was "when Alyssa eats good." I asked Hayley about it and she said her counselor had asked her to make a list of things that make her happy. Seeing that listed as one of them really opened my eyes to the amount of pain and worry I have caused others. The fact that this is something I wasn't supposed to see added even more to the reality of pain I have caused.

◆ ◆ ◆

Yesterday turned out to be quite an unusual trip to Mr. Freeze for me. Hayley had told me from the beginning that when she took me to Mr. Freeze I would have to order something other than my usual, Wow Cow(which contains only 10 calories an ounce, no sugar and zero calories from fat). Well when we walked up to the window to place my usual order, Hayley raised her voice and told the employee not to give it to me. Hayley actually created quite a scene when she walked away threatening she would make me walk home if I continued with my order. So I ordered my usual Wow Cow by myself and walked to the back parking lot where her car was waiting(I knew she would never leave without me). Her explanation for not leaving was that she didn't want to give me the satisfaction of walking home as a way to burn calories. The whole incident was humorous. However, I'm sure the employee and customers nearby were a little uncomfortable. As if that wasn't enough, when we returned to my house Hayley was "put in charge" by my mother to make sure I ate something for dinner. I told her I would make a tuna salad and lettuce sandwich. I set out the ingredients, made the sandwich and placed the tuna and lettuce back in the fridge. As I did that, Hayley walked over to my sandwich, pulled off the top slice of bread and discovered that there was only lettuce. My punishment: extra tuna because I tried to get away with eating just bread and lettuce.

◆ ◆ ◆

Today I went with Christina and Hayley to Hometown Buffet for a late lunch. I ate so much food. It was ridiculous. I don't understand how after all that I ate, I wasn't full. Afterwards I felt terrible, I didn't deserve to eat as much as I did and I know that I'm going to end up paying for it.

More than ever I had the biggest urge to throw up, but I knew it wasn't an option. Thanks God for watching out for me and for giving me family and friends who are constantly watching every move I make. If they didn't make my health such a huge priority, I would have easily found a way to relieve myself. Although I desperately wanted to, I couldn't. I know it's for the best.

◆ ◆ ◆

Throwing up is probably one of the worst feelings, especially when it's forced. I can't even understand what has made me do it before and why I constantly have the urge to still do it. The whole idea is utterly disgusting. You gag several times until you finally can get it to come out, your throat hurts the whole day, the taste left in your mouth is repulsive, and sometimes if you are "lucky" enough to get rid of all the food, you puke out blood. It scares me to think of the damage it can do to your internal organs after just a few times. I can't wait until I have my own children one day. The thought that I have the power to ruin those dreams terrifies me.

◆ ◆ ◆

I know my family and friends are watching out for me because of how much they care. I appreciate that, I really do, but sometimes it can be so irritating and frustrating. Do you know what it's like to have people question what you ate for breakfast, lunch and dinner? To be watched as you eat? To be followed when you go to the bathroom? To have special rules established dealing with food and privacy issues? I feel like a prisoner. Even with everyone being there for me, I feel more alone than ever because the mental side of my eating disorder sets me apart from anyone else.

When I was around food that I would not allow myself to eat, I panicked. You could even go as far to say that I went crazy. My mom loves to bake desserts. She would make a batch of cookies or puppy chow on a regular basis to lie on the kitchen counter for our family and friends to enjoy. I did not like this. I would belt out nasty comments, and beg her to stop by telling her she was inconsiderate. I saw it as a challenge. How long could it sit there without me eating any of it? If I gave in, I would blame it on my mom. It was torture when I would walk in the door from school already tired and starving, and then smell the aroma of chocolate chip cookies, knowing I would never allow myself to indulge.

I remember one time specifically after a counseling appointment. My parents ordered pizza and bread sticks for dinner. I was furious. I could not understand why they would do that to me. I became so anxious and frustrated I had to literally leave the house. I got in my car, crying foolishly and drove around. I felt a need to run away from my problems. Times like this I would either work out, or go to Hayley's house.

◆ ◆ ◆

Dinner time was always a struggle. When I was hungry, I would stand in front of the pantry with the door wide open and stare in helplessness. I felt the need to ask my parents constantly what I should eat. Why, I am not sure, considering their input was never taken. My mom always cooked what most would consider a nutritious home-cooked meal, but no matter how good it might have looked, I refused to allow myself to eat it.

When I was forced to eat with my family, I insisted on using a salad plate. After countless arguments, I got away with it because my parents realized it was better for me to eat something than nothing at all. Even though my plate was much smaller, I had a rule. I could not allow myself to fill my plate for I could not be trusted with a normal serving size. I cut everything in half. Dinner almost always led to disagreement between my parents and I.

◆ ◆ ◆

This summer I have decided to start reading more. I have never been an avid reader but I feel that reading may help spiritually and build self confidence. I really enjoy reading books about girls journeys through eating disorders. It proves that I'm not alone and that is more comforting than anything else.

I found that reading became a sense of inspiration throughout my recovery. Although difficult to find, my favorites were personal diaries and stories related to eating disorders. I felt so alone throughout this stage and reading stories that expressed my same feelings gave me encouragement and hope. I can remember one afternoon at a bookstore with my mom. We grabbed a bunch of books and sat at a table. I began rummaging through the pages of a particular book that caught my eye. While skimming through the pages one by one I became nauseated. I felt weak and panicked because of the visuals the words created in my mind. I had to put the book down, because it was way too painful to read at that point in my life. Several months later while at the public library, I picked it up again and read through the excruciating pain the author suffered through and still does to this day. I am glad I read that book. It depicts the exact mind of an anorexic/bulimic. I am also glad that I waited to read it.

I have always been interested in psychology for as long as I can remember. After all I have been through, my interest in this career has only increased.

◆ ◆ ◆

Throughout this short amount of time, I am now seeing the physical effects of my eating habits on my body. I thought the dryness of my hair and the amount of hair I lost in the shower could be solved by switching conditioners. Now I realize that it was due to the lack of protein and minerals my body needed. I noticed that I had grown more hair on my face, arms, and stomach. I had lost a healthy looking color to my skin and looked emaciated. My eyes appeared sunken in and I had bags under my eyes. I was always cold and exhausted. Now that I have brought needed minerals back into my body, I am slowly seeing my body transform into being healthy again.

Although nothing could surpass the emotional strain of the eating disorder, the physical aspects were nowhere near easy. Sure, in the beginning I felt great. I loved feeling thin and when I made it through the day eating only celery and carrots, I felt exhilarated. I even felt like I had more energy. Of course that changed quickly. I slowly started feeling tired and exhausted. It became hard to stay awake in school. All I wanted to do was lay around because I had no energy for anything else. Little things such as walking up stairs became tiring, and no matter what I could never keep my body warm. My hands and feet were always freezing, they were ghostly white at times and I became known as the girl always in a hooded sweatshirt despite the temperature surroundings. I was miserable. Every few weeks or so I went to the tanning salon for the sole purpose of hiding the monotone color to my skin. I didn't even have the energy to have fun or laugh when I was with my friends. Exercising became unbearable at times but I pushed myself knowing that it needed to be done. On Friday nights out with my friends, all I could think about was when I was going to go home and exercise. If I spent the night somewhere, I would have to work out double the next day.

Physical symptoms I experienced:

-I would wake up in the middle of the night, freezing cold yet dripping in sweat nearly every night.

-It took hours to fall asleep at night and even then, I woke up tossing and turning. I worried about everything. If I did not lay food for the next day out on the counter before I went to bed, I could not sleep. Not only had I become a semi-insomniac but I also fit the description for chronic fatigue syndrome.

-Sleeping was uncomfortable. While I was laying down, my bones stuck out to the degree it hurt to sleep.

-I suffered from anticipatory anxiety, which was constant.

-My heart at times felt as if it were beating much faster, and I occasionally would become short of breath, making it difficult to breathe.

-I felt dizzy often.

-I was always freezing, my skin tone lost a healthy looking color, turning almost a whitish yellow. I even wore gloves during most of my classes because my hands were so cold and my coat remained on during the first half of the day.

-My hair began to fall out in the shower and throughout the day in greater amounts than usual. Not only that, it became dry and brittle.

-I grew a thick coat of hair over my body. (Called Lanugo, a symptom of being underweight) I started shaving and trimming my face in an effort to hide it.

-Sometimes I would lose feeling in my arms or legs. I wouldn't be able to move and I felt very weak. This happened during classes when I would change positions at my desk.

-My periods stopped. (Called Amenorrhea) Amenorrhea can cause infertility when older.

-Depression. I would consider it physical, because it was physically draining.

-Constipation…as soon as I began to eat normal food such as pizza, I spent more time in the bathroom than I had in six months. Whatever I ate came out more quickly than I could digest it.

◆ ◆ ◆

Anorexia and bulimia are two words I learned about in school health classes since fourth grade. Even a year ago I can remember wondering to myself what on earth could possess someone to induce vomiting and stop eating. To me food was something I could never imagine wanting to refuse and the thought of throwing up, made me feel weak and nauseated. In a million years I never would have believed that my relationship with food would change and form into an eating disorder. I now realize that having an eating disorder is not based on the little or big amount that you indulge in, but instead the obsession you build for food.

◆ ◆ ◆

What provoked this change in my eating habits and loss of self confidence? This question has been brought up numerous times with my counselor, family and friends and even now I don't think I have an answer. I can't blame my actions based on an event or the people in my life. As much as I want to, I can't. I feel like I need to be the perfect example of how a daughter and sister should be. Developing an eating disorder is not a good start. I sometimes feel that it's easier to just agree when people suggest Rory may have added to it. Yes I did want to feel beautiful and perfect for him, but now I realize something. I <u>was</u> perfect in his eyes before I started to lose weight and I would be despite my weight. He loved me for the person I am on the inside. I am to blame for this eating disorder. I don't know how I can accept and forgive myself because I have hurt so many people, including me.

◆ ◆ ◆

Today my mom and Hayley conducted a little experiment. On my driveway Hayley told me to draw with chalk what I believed the shape of my body was. Afterwards, I laid down and she drew the actual outline with a different color. Although her outline was much smaller, it is still hard to be convinced of the point they were trying to prove. I do know that what I see in the mirror is a distorted image. Or is it?

◆ ◆ ◆

I was also informed today that on July 1 my family and I are attending a support group located at the an eating disorder treatment center in Sylvania. My family has been greatly affected by my eating situation and they believe that talking openly will help with recovery for not just me but them as well.

◆ ◆ ◆

I did it! I accomplished one of my goals. I went with Hayley to Mr. Freeze today and ordered a regular ice cream sundae. Not knowing the exact calorie content is frightening but hopefully I will have enough confidence to do it again. It tasted wonderful, but I felt so guilty.

Sadly, despite my progress and weight gain I was never able to order regular ice cream again that summer from Mr. Freeze.

◆ ◆ ◆

The amount of food I have eaten today is revolting. Since I changed my eating habits, candy, chocolate, meat and potato chips were on what I considered a poison list. Well today I just starting binging on bite-size candy bars and candy. I couldn't stop and I can't believe I let myself eat like that. I feel like that incident has ruined my image completely. Why did I turn to food for comfort? I feel like eating is the best solution when I'm upset, lonely or anxious. I crave it as something other than its purpose.

♦ ♦ ♦

I keep trying to remind myself that a number on a scale doesn't make up who I am. My weight shouldn't control my mind, but it does. I wish I could see how much I have gained so I can feel in control again. I hate not feeling in control of my weight, and meals for the day. I try to keep the calories I consume early in the day low because I never know what I might eat later on. What if I am with my friends and they decide to go for ice cream or make some popcorn? If I save extra calories for later just in case, I won't feel as guilty. I'm still always considering everything I put into my mouth. If I decide to indulge in a snack I can't help but feel guilty and preplan a workout or healthier meals for the next day. I shouldn't have to think about what I'm going to eat for the next day. I need to improve on this.

♦ ♦ ♦

I think it's hilarious that my parents won't leave me home for more than five minutes. If they are leaving, they make sure I will be with Hayley so I don't throw up. It's good on their part because I know that if they left me alone I would throw up what I eat and I don't want to do that. It scares me to think about wanting to do it.

♦ ♦ ♦

I feel like I'm standing in the middle of quick sand. The more I struggle to get out of this mess I'm in, the lower I start to sink.

◆ ◆ ◆

Definitely had a fat day today. I couldn't stand looking at my thighs and sides. I feel like I have so much to pinch and grab at. I knew I had to gain weight and though without a scale I can tell I have. Now the weight I needed to gain no longer feels needed. My mom keeps reassuring me that I'm starting to look healthier again. Did I honestly not look good before or are they lying about my figure now? I guess there is nothing I can do but trust my family and friends.

◆ ◆ ◆

Well it has been confirmed...Mary Kate Olsen is in a treatment center for anorexia. I don't understand it. She was always so tiny and gorgeous. If someone like her can have low self confidence about her image then I can only imagine how many girls are struggling themselves. Eating disorders are serious and it upsets me that the media can turn it all into one big joke and put her down for it. At least she has the courage to want to get better. Everyone should be more aware of the symptoms and there should be more support groups for patients of eating disorders. Schools concentrate on drug and alcohol abuse. The number of teenagers with eating disorders is continuing to increase steadily and school systems should start to look at image problems as a focal point as well. People can die of eating disorders too. It doesn't just happen in movies. I found that out the hard way. Maybe if they were taken more seriously, no one else would have to suffer as much as I have.

◆ ◆ ◆

It's sad how I know the serving size, calories, grams of fat, etc. you name it, for almost all products imaginable. Hayley used to always ask me when she would pull something out of the cupboards for the content while she checked to see if I was right. The other night Christina just kept asking me about different foods. I believe they find it fascinating and odd how I have memorized them all. If I were on a game show all about food, I am convinced I would win hands down. That is really sad.

◆ ◆ ◆

Once again my mind is fighting. It can only be described as long battle of a tug of war and I'm stuck in the middle. I know I should be eating and not worrying. I know what I did before wasn't healthy and I started to look too skinny. One side of my mind accepts that I have gained weight. The other is a different story. When the positive side of my mind seems to be taking control and gaining strength, the negative side kicks in. Maybe I'm eating too much? Maybe I should cut back on calories? Maybe I didn't look too skinny before? It's a battle every day that is growing old. I can only hope that the positive side continues to grow and eventually gains complete strength.

"I'll do whatever I have to do to get you better, even if it means you'll temporarily hate me."

The Last Straw

Janet Biederman

In May 2004 Alyssa and I went shopping at the mall. She had been hiding her frail body underneath layers of clothes which became painfully obvious when she tried on a size zero pair of pants. As she walked out of the dressing room and she stood in front of me, they literally fell off her hips. Her quest to become thin had taken a serious toll on her body. I felt hopeless and tormented. Weeks later after we opened our pool for the summer, I was sickened by what I saw. Alyssa attempted to cover up her silhouette with a towel, but I got enough of a glimpse to know what I needed to do. To think just a year ago, she had a body anyone would envy. I bought a scale for the day and got rid of it. Ninety-seven pounds. This is it.

"I'll do whatever I have to do to get you better even if it means you'll temporarily hate me."

◆ ◆ ◆

In my frantic search for an eating disorder treatment facility, I found the answer to my prayers. I found a website link to a treatment *center that specialized in treating eating disorders just twenty miles up the road.*

My husband and I sat down with Alyssa and showed her the information about the treatment center. I called for information and talked with her about our last-ditch effort to save her life. Without hesitation, she agreed. I was told once they received her on-line registration, there would be a possible wait list. We didn't have time to wait. I knew we had to act immediately.

◆ ◆ ◆

While out shopping with Alyssa the next day, we found ourselves driving toward the treatment center. We were having a discussion in the car about how good everything will be again once she gets the help she needs when Alyssa asked to drive by the facility. All I had was an address and by the grace of God we found it. Just seeing the facility was life changing. We couldn't get in, but there was something magical about her just seeing the center that brought tears to her eyes. "Mom," she said, "I want to get better." We held each other in the car for what seemed like an hour. As we pulled out of the parking lot, she said she wanted to do everything she could do to avoid going there. As much as I wanted to believe her, I knew I couldn't.

There was silence the rest of the way home. If I could not get her into the treatment center immediately, I would set rules and follow plans as if she was in a treatment center. Obviously, not with the same expertise or medical care, but nevertheless, I would try. One mistake, it's over.

◆ ◆ ◆

As a family we sat down and went over the new house rules. Most of the rules seemed elementary. In an effort to help Alyssa, we were forced to take away her privacy. We made her eat all of her meals in front of us. She was not allowed to use the restroom for an hour after she ate and then had to leave the door cracked open. She was no longer permitted to exercise and absolutely could not be left home alone. As terrible as this all sounds, she willingly participated. She wanted to get better and slowly but surely, she is.

I am sure there were times Alyssa felt like a prisoner in her own home. Truthfully, it felt that way for us as well. It was our job as parents to do everything we could to save our daughter before it was too late. We became babysitters as well as parents. We planned our nights out around hers. Her brother, Tyler, and Hayley were a tremendous help.

We had to face the reality that recovery would not be easy. It would require the utmost patience. Baby steps were required. She needed to trust we would not expect too much too soon and we needed to trust she would try to understand it was okay to eat and feed her body properly.

I took it upon myself to learn as much as I could about anorexia and other eating disorders. I was disappointed, however, by the lack of books that dealt with the true feelings and confusion in the mind of an anorexic or sufferer of an eating disorder. Knowledge is power and I thrived on obtaining as much knowledge on the subject as possible. I needed to find a book for Alyssa to relate to. One that would prove to her she was not alone and would validate her feelings and thoughts. One that would allow her to accept the fact recovery was possible. Finding such a book was difficult.

While shopping at a bookstore, I came across a book that helped us both. It helped me realize just how confused the mind of an eating disorder victim becomes. It also proved to me that from the outside looking in, a person may not always be as perfect as they appear.

"The truth is no matter what is said about food these days, I will take it the wrong way."

More Journal Entries, 2004

Today I was talked into going to Greenfield Village with my family and grandparents. We were there all day and as lunchtime came along we stopped at a pavilion to eat. At the lunch stand, I noticed my choices were limited. Fat, grease, and more fat. I looked up at my dad but his response was not one that I wanted to hear. He told me I had to eat something. My mom and I walked around trying to find a healthier option but after walking in a circle, nothing was found. I ended up having to eat a quarter of a cheeseburger and a few of my mom's french fries. I could see my grandpa (who has no knowledge of my eating disorder) stare at me in disgust as I compulsively patted the burger and fries with a handful of napkins, making sure there wasn't a speck of grease left.

◆ ◆ ◆

I'm scared. I am afraid that my anorexic behavior is going to change into a compulsive eating disorder. Books my mom and I have read talk about this a lot. Lately I have been going on binges where I eat food just to eat. The food I deprived my body of before, I can't stop thinking about. When I decide to help myself to a cookie or some pretzels, I can't just stop at one or a handful. God, please be with me to make smart choices. I'm afraid that I will begin the cycle all over again.

◆ ◆ ◆

I hate this. Why does what go on in my mind have to cause so many problems? There is no reason why my whole family should be arguing with each other because of the way I react to a simple comment about food. My mom tries so hard to make me happy and make this situation better, but sometimes I wish she would just realize that I need to help myself. She tries to be super mom and solve problems that no mother can solve for their daughter. I know she is just being protective and trying to help, but sometimes it just makes me feel worse.

I refused to eat lunch with the family today and later started randomly snacking on different foods. My mom took action. She asked if I was just eating to eat or if I was hungry. She wants to make sure that when I do eat, I put good, nutritious food in my body. You'd think she would just be happy I am eating something. Although my mom obviously does not want me to move from one slump to another, when she made that comment today, it scared me. I felt as if she was telling me the food I just ate went straight to my hips. I haven't exercised for a few weeks, but tonight I went running and did other exercises for an hour and a half. This created a major uproar in my family. I feel like now I should start restricting my calorie intake again. I know my overreaction to her comments is what got me in this mess from the beginning and now I am starting to feel how I felt more than six months ago; fat…again.

♦   ♦   ♦

My parents started arguing about how my mom dealt with the situation earlier today. Why does it seem that the only time my parents disagree is when it's about me? I hate always feeling like the culprit. I already feel somewhat "mental" enough and when they argue about me, I can't help but feel worse. The truth is, no matter what is said about food these days, I will take it the wrong way.

♦   ♦   ♦

Yay! Today I showed strength and confidence in myself and it felt great. I ate an amount of food that I was uncomfortable with again this afternoon. My parents were gone and my brother was intensely involved in his video games in his room. I knew it was my chance. I could end the guilt right then and there with just a simple flush of the toilet. I walked in, shut the door behind me, took position, slowly stuck my finger down my throat, and then paused. I removed my finger and asked myself what I would accomplish if I did do it. The answer was plain and simple. Nothing! It wouldn't make me a better person, friend or more attractive. It would, however, portray my weakness and categorize me as another statistic I do not want to be. At that moment, I stood up and walked away. As silly as it sounds, I cannot stop smiling.

♦   ♦   ♦

This morning I woke up with a sense of inspiration. It's like things are suddenly starting to become more clear. This feeling of comfort and hope came from none other than my friend, Dan. Last night Dan and I were driving in my car on the way to pick up one of our friends. On the way, we started talking about my eating disorder. Throughout my issues with eating, I learned that he had dealt with similar issues nearly four years ago. He began talking to me about it and he started to cry. He was trying to fight back the tears and I felt awkward. I didn't know exactly what to say, but I realized I did not have to say anything. He knew everything that was going through my mind because he had gone through it too. This just comforted me even more. Upon picking up our friend, we rode in silence until later than night when Dan came back to my house with me and we ended up talking about it most of the night. It was amazing how similar our stories were. Everything he felt was exactly the way I feel now. Hayley and my parents have been there for me to talk to unconditionally. However, it was so therapeutic talking to someone who had actually been through the same thing. Especially since he is one of my closest friends.

◆ ◆ ◆

This morning I woke up and thought about how I was going to plan my calories for the day. I couldn't focus on anything else. It was my dad's birthday and I would be expected to eat dinner with the family. My mom was making spaghetti and ravioli. I couldn't figure out a way to disappoint my dad and get away with it. As much as I thought about it all day, for some reason my attitude about it completely changed when my dad got home from work. I willingly ate spaghetti and even ate quite a bit of the chocolate cookie dough ice cream pie for dessert. I still can't believe I allowed myself to eat all that fat. Actually, come to think of it, I ate a whole lot of it. And the rest of the night, I didn't even have a cloud of guilt in my mind and I still don't. I wonder where this new sense of enlightenment came from, because it changed over the course of a few hours. Wow! Did I miss the feeling of being able to enjoy some-

thing without feeling guilty. Hopefully I can hold on to this momentary bliss. Mom had commented earlier in the day that sharing the meal with the family is one of the best presents I could give him at this time. It felt like more than just a gift to my dad, but to me as well.

◆ ◆ ◆

I didn't have to go to that support group tonight. My mom called to confirm the time and she was informed that the patients rarely come. It is usually just centered around the parents and brothers/sisters. What a relief, I was dreading having to share my feelings to a group of strangers.

◆ ◆ ◆

I love to finally feel like people understand. Tonight I was at Dan's with some people and they ordered a pizza. Some of the guys questioned why I was not eating. I told them I wasn't hungry, and it was the truth. I also told them I had already eaten, that part wasn't true. One of them tried persuading me to eat, but Dan understood and told them not to worry about it, I would eat later. It was a relief to have someone trying to make me feel more comfortable.

◆ ◆ ◆

The reason I barely ate today was simply because I didn't feel good, not because I was concerned about calories. Even though I wasn't hungry, I looked at it as a plus because I have eaten a lot of fatty foods lately and I could stand to go light for a day or two.

◆   ◆   ◆

Two weeks ago my mom told me that she had bought me something that would be given to me in exactly two weeks provided I eat three meals a day and do not throw up. Yes I know, it was a bribe, but I stuck with it and was given a new comforter for my bed! She told me that every two weeks as long as I stick to the rules I will get something small. It seriously helps motivate me, as sadly as that may sound.

As if that was not bad enough, my parents tried controlling my social life with food. I was told if I did not eat a meal, I could not leave for the weekend or go out for the night with my friends. In fact, I couldn't go to the store tonight until I ate four bites of steak.

◆   ◆   ◆

My grandpa now knows about my eating disorder. He left a message on the answering machine the other night for my dad saying that he had been meaning to talk to him about something important and to call right away no matter what time we got in. The first thing that came to mind with my family was that it concerned my grandpa's health...not expecting it would actually be about mine. My grandpa expressed his feelings of concern to my dad about my weight when he was in town and the little I ate, including how I patted all the grease possible out of the quarter of a cheeseburger I ate. My parents had no choice but to tell him he was right and it has been a battle in the family for the last half of the year and we are working on recovery. I'm thankful that my grandpa showed so much concern...I wonder what he would have done if he had seen me weeks prior at my worst.

♦ ♦ ♦

I haven't experienced the satisfaction of stepping on a scale for nearly a month until yesterday. I went to visit Ohio University for a college tour and on our way home we stopped for a bite to eat. As we were leaving and my dad was paying the bill, I noticed a scale that showed your weight and "decoded your dreams." I pulled out the required dime out of my purse, took a deep breath and stepped on the scale. I only caught a quick glimpse because my mom appeared from around the corner. The quick glimpse I caught put a damper on my day. I knew I had gained weight but seeing the number on the scale makes me feel defeated and not in control. The rest of the way home I devised a plan to exercise while my parents attended my brother's baseball game. What they don't know can't hurt, and besides I ate a lot of unhealthy food the past few days with my family. I'm not just talking onion rings and chicken, but a dairy queen blizzard! Well, my plan fell through when Hayley called and we decided to go over to our friend Mark's house for the night. I think God had that one planned. But while upstairs in the bathroom at his house I noticed he had a scale! I couldn't stop staring at the scale the whole time I peed, trying to talk myself out of using it. I gave in and stood on it. It showed I weighed a little less than the scale in the restaurant. In fact according to this scale I only gained two pounds since my physical...somehow I don't think that's right because I feel like I have put on much more than that, especially with the change in my eating habits. Oh yes and to make things even more humorous, I ended up kissing Mark last night. Yeah, probably not one of the best decisions I've ever made. He is one of my good friends. Haha oh well, I don't have anything else to say about that one.

◆ ◆ ◆

I had a dream last night that was so vivid. I was at some eating disorder support group and was completely humiliated when my weight was said aloud in front of a huge audience. I ran out of the room practically in tears while someone followed behind me. We started talking and he understood my feelings completely. We talked throughout the session about our problems and it scared me to hear everyone talking so openly about their situations. As he walked me out to meet my parents, a group of the other attendees formed a line and circled around me shouting E-A-T, E-A-T. It was by far one of the most bizarre dreams I have ever had. I think it's telling me that it's still far from over…lets hope it's just acting as a reminder to continue on the path I've started.

◆ ◆ ◆

I just binged on probably the most fattening ice cream possible. What's worse is that it is 11:30 at night. Why couldn't I have just gone to bed? There is absolutely no purpose in eating at this time. Oh well, I am already in a down mood. I will just have to work it off tomorrow.

◆ ◆ ◆

"A person with an eating disorder can be a master of deception. Not because they purposely lie and think they can get away with it, but because they actually believe the stories they tell. When I read about the binge eating instances that Alyssa refers to throughout this book, I cringe. Not because I picture her eating a gallon of ice cream, a couple pieces of cake and two slices of pizza, but because I know the truth. They weren't actual binges

at all, but to her they felt like it. Like the false perception she had of her body, she also associated eating ice cream or other forbidden foods as binges regardless of the amount she actually ate. No matter how much I try to help, I always feel like I say the wrong thing or my words are misinterpreted."—Janet Biederman

◆   ◆   ◆

I saw what I would consider one of the most depressing yet hopeful movies tonight. Hayley and I went to see The Notebook. I want the love that was displayed in the movie. It was so intense and pure, I felt like I was experiencing it myself. Maybe because I have. What I had with Rory felt so real…in fact, so real that I can still feel it. I remember each moment spent together as if it were only hours ago.

I wrote a letter last night for Rory summing up all my thoughts and emotions. I have to admit that it was pretty darn good. It was the easiest letter I have ever written because I was able to release all the emotion I had bottled up over the past few months and the feelings came straight from the heart. This afternoon I took the letter and a burned cd he had once given me with one song on it. He had given me the cd with a note expressing his feelings when we had gotten in an argument some time ago. I knew he would be at work and since no one else was home, I slipped it in the mailbox. Did he call tonight? No…and man does that hurt. I guess watching a tear wrenching chick flick just fit the mood of the night. It's more difficult than it sounds-reality that is. Wouldn't you expect after writing a sentimental and powerful letter in which you spill out your heart to the person you shared everything with that there would at least be some return action on their part? Perhaps a telephone call at least? If I can do the right thing and express my feelings, why can't he at least try?

◆ ◆ ◆

Hayley and I went to visit Ryan tonight. Ryan is a mutual friend of ours who was involved in a tragic automobile accident during our sophomore year. Visiting Ryan gives me a sense of hope and inspiration. Every time I leave his house I remember what the meaning of life is really about. Why worry about the small things when I should be thanking God for all that I have? It's funny...when he first got in the accident seeing him in his current state was emotionally painful, but now when I leave I can't help but smile. I smile because of the progress he has made and the strength his family has to encourage him. I can only imagine how painful it must be to wake up every morning to a son whose life has changed forever and there is nothing left to do but have hope.

◆ ◆ ◆

On Tuesday Hayley and I have interviews at Hospice. Provided everything goes well, we will attend a three-hour orientation next weekend and begin volunteering soon. I think the experience will be one not forgotten. I am hoping to be able to take a new sense on life out from volunteering and to help take everything else off my mind.

◆ ◆ ◆

I was really looking forward to going up to Michigan for Brett's graduation party tomorrow, but unfortunately it's not going to work out. As pathetic as it may sound, the only positive is the relief of him not seeing me. I haven't seen Brett and his friends for over a month and since then I feel like I have put on an excess of weight. Gosh I hate feeling so up and down about everything. If I don't eat, I'm unhappy, so then I eat...but once again I'm unhappy because I ate. I wish I could just make up my mind and stick to one feeling. I really wanted to go running today but I know my mom would not have been too keen on the idea since it would be two days of exercising in a row. I had to stick to the silent crunches and leg lifts in the privacy of my room today. I did eat a slice of cheese pizza tonight and two bread sticks from Papa Johns and oh did it taste so good. The best part was that I ate it without even thinking about it. Ok...I take that back. Now I am starting to think about it, but at least at the time I didn't.

◆ ◆ ◆

Numb. That's the best word I can use to describe how I feel right now. I thought I was experiencing every emotion earlier tonight. I thought my heart felt like it was torn apart, then I thought I was angry, and then guilty and annoyed. But now that I think about it, I don't really think I feel anything. Right now I feel incapable of crying. My heart feels so empty that I don't know how I feel anymore. I feel nothing and I'm trying to figure out whether that's a good or a bad thing. One minute I want nothing more than for Rory to be back in my life or make some effort, and another minute I think of how I don't need him there because of how full my heart is becoming with love from other people. It's a cycle...empty...full...empty...full...what will it be like tomorrow?

♦ ♦ ♦

I wish I possessed the strength and courage like the characters displayed on tv and in movies. Like when a man/woman runs up to their love and makes a daring move. When they pour out their emotions and kiss the other without warning and unsure of what their reaction will be. Perhaps that's why I become so engrossed in tv shows like Dawson's Creek and the OC...because I know I don't have the strength to recreate their actions. I lack the confidence unlike the characters on television. I love watching these shows and become so involved as if it were my own soap opera. But when I think about it, soap opera's are drama, and the little drama I experience first hand in life is more than enough for me...at least for now. Until then, I will stick to the fear of rejection as an incentive to not make a daring move.

♦ ♦ ♦

My parents left this morning so it was the perfect opportunity to go for a nice run. I got back before they returned home but Hayley had already called and found out from my brother that I had gone running. It sucks to feel like I need to hide when I exercise from her. Right now I'm just trying to stay in shape. I guess to Hayley it's just not an "Alyssa" thing to do. Perhaps because usually on Saturday mornings I would lay in bed watching reruns of television shows. After I got off the phone with her, I proceeded downstairs to do some crunches and tone defining exercises. Not too far into the workout, once my parents got home, Hayley called again and told my mom I had gone for a run. When my mom found me in the basement exercising again, this created some problems. You know it's pathetic when your family is actually getting on your case about exercising. Usually parents would praise their children and encourage them to get in shape and stay healthy. Well I guess things aren't exactly normal right now. I mean I get congratulated for every pound I gain. To them it's like hearing the greatest news in the world...how many people these days view gaining weight as a positive thing? Society views it so differently. I guess my situation may be a little different compared to the majority of people right now.

One night, I went running outside around the neighborhood. I was quite aways from my house and the sky was quickly getting darker and the air cooler. I kept at a steady pace while sprinkles of rain dropped from the sky. I started to feel dizzy and light headed. My hands tingled from my fingers up to my arm. My legs felt numb and I was losing feeling throughout my body every few minutes. I started to get scared. I was afraid of passing out on the side of the road and not being discovered for a while. How long would it take for someone to drive by and discover my unfortunate fall? Despite my pessimistic sense of fear, I continued running. I did not stop. I would not stop. I would run until I felt satisfied with myself.

◆ ◆ ◆

As much as everything has improved, I know things still are not right. When I wake up in the morning, my thoughts still center around food. I don't want to think about food first when I wake up. Why can't I focus my attention on how I'm going to spend my day or what I'm going to watch on tv like most teenagers?

My mind was constantly centered around burning calories. I once read that approximately 1,500 steps burn one hundred calories. In order to keep track of how many calories I burned during the school day, I actually began counting how many steps it took to get from one class to another. I worked as an office aide the second semester of my junior year and I thrived on the errands I had to run knowing I was burning calories with each note I delivered. Working in the office required another test of my power of control. Food was always offered to the office aides and my ability to deny such food gave me a sense of strength.

◆ ◆ ◆

I really wanted to work out today but I knew I wouldn't be able to get away with it. I know my family and Hayley are just watching out for me, but it is so annoying. I hate that they get upset at me for working out and running. I try to do it without them knowing, but they always seem to find out. It's pathetic that I fear getting caught. It seems like whenever Hayley calls on the phone, she interrupts my workouts. It is hard to disguise the heavy breathing and I am forced to listen to her lovely speeches berating me. She is constantly breathing down my neck about it. If I had never had an eating disorder, she wouldn't think twice about it. Unfortunately, because I have lied before, they don't believe me when I tell them my thoughts don't center around burning calories.

When I worked out in the house, I enjoyed working out in my room the most. The full length mirror in my room was in just the perfect place when I began my workouts. I ran in place directly in front of the mirror critiquing my body. I usually worked out in a sports bra and underwear allowing me to judge each curve and "weakness" even closer. In the mirror, I saw someone I did not like and a body I despised. I saw someone different in the mirror's reflection. Working out in front of the mirror pushed me to work harder. My workout usually consisted of running in place for 20 minutes if not more, crunches, and thigh trimming routines I read about in a magazine, however no matter what I did, it never felt like enough.

◆ ◆ ◆

I have learned to hate going to Chili's with my family for dinner. Thankfully we don't eat there for dinner every Monday evening like we used to. Don't get me wrong. It is not that I don't like Chili's. In fact, I love their food. Unfortunately, my family always orders the bottomless chips and salsa as an appetizer. So what's the problem? I can't control myself. I feel anxious because I know it is right in front of me and I can't stand to watch them chow down and enjoy it while I deny myself the privilege. I tell myself I'm not going to eat more than a couple, but once I start, I can't stop. When I go to restaurants and there is an excess of food sitting right across the table, I'm out of my safety zone. I feel powerless. Like the bowl of chips or the basket of bread is a magnetic field pulling me closer and revealing my weakness. Tonight I told myself beforehand, I was only going to get a salad because I had previously eaten a bowl of cereal. Yeah, I ordered my salad, ate that, but then I also had a few too many handfuls of chips. Not to mention I also had a few bites of my mom's rice and a piece of her chicken. I wasn't full when I left at all, but I felt terrible. I feel like I'm gaining too much weight and I'm eating more food than I should. But at the same time, I know overall I don't eat that much throughout the day. I just feel like I do. Because I nearly starved myself before and restricted my calories so heavily I'm gaining the weight back a lot quicker. I know I need to accept it because it is healthier, but looking in the mirror now I look so much different than two months ago. I miss what I used to see. Yeah I know I was starting to look disgustingly skinny, but it's hard to watch that feeling of controlling my thinness disappear down the drain. My biggest fear is the weight gaining not stopping. I just keep telling myself that once I find the number of calories I need a day, my body will maintain a healthy weight.

◆ ◆ ◆

More than anything, I love swinging on the swing set at the park. Nothing relaxes my mind more than the wind blowing through my hair and feeling the gentle breeze that touches my face as I swing back and forth. I love to reminisce about the days when there were no worries. The days I could eat as many candy bars I wanted on Halloween night or any day for that matter. The days when I never worried about my weight. The days when high school graduation and college seemed years away. The days when I got the jitters during a game of truth or dare or when I got the nerve to run up to my "crush" at recess and gave him a peck on the cheek before quickly and anxiously scurrying away. The days before I learned how wonderful it feels to be in love and how much it hurts to have my heart broken. Perhaps that's why I love to swing. It sends me back to my childhood and days of naive innocence-before I even learned the true definition of sex. When I'm swinging, I'm in my own world. I control how high I fly and how long I decide to be taken away from this crazy, mixed-up world. As soon as I jump off, reality sets in. If I could only go back to my childhood, my worries would be over.

◆ ◆ ◆

I love shopping. I swear it sometimes scares me because of how quickly it turns into an instant pick me up. Oh well, it won't be a prob-

lem. I hate spending my own money so if mom doesn't buy it, it stays on the rack. My mom and dad have been weary about buying clothes for me lately. They hate the fact that even the smallest sizes at most stores are baggy on me and don't fit. In fact, today my mom told me they would not buy me any more clothes until I gained weight.

♦ ♦ ♦

You think you can just walk out of my life more quickly than you came into it? You think after two years you can get away with not even so much as a proper goodbye? You think that avoiding me doesn't hurt? I don't know if either you're just that strong, or I am all the more weak. But I do know that I can't let everything just disappear between us. The way you are just pushing me away makes me question everything. What was I? Some damn conquest to see how long you can date a girl, fall in love and then walk away from her? We were best friends, not just boyfriend and girlfriend.

♦ ♦ ♦

I realized that my period still has not started this month. I'm just over a week late. I just can't figure out why. Right before I started birth control my period was two and a half weeks late. Of course I freaked out even though at the time I was still a virgin. That was the beginning of December. My period had always been consistent. I started in sixth grade and I could pinpoint the start of my period each month to the hour. When it started so late in December, I was curious, but once it started I forgot about it and began taking my birth control pills which forced me to have a period regularly. After Rory and I broke up, my mom decided to take me off the pills. My period failed to return for some time. I now realize why I was late before and why I am not starting, but I am frustrated. I have been eating lately. Maybe I'm not fully back to my proper weight like I thought. I guess we will just have to wait and see what happens. Normally the lack of a period would scare the hell out of me. Now knowing that there is no possible way I could be pregnant, I don't miss it one bit.

◆ ◆ ◆

"Oh I've got a crush." Haha…ok so I really miss Rory. But I think what I miss so much was the level of comfort. Even though I spend so much time thinking of him, I have developed little crushes on some other boys. Yeah, I made out with two of them this summer. The one lives two hours away, but I will admit my attraction to him is not just about his cute looks but the thought of replaying him as the boy from spring break. In my heart, I know it's not about wanting a relationship again, but about enjoying the attention. I wouldn't want anything to happen with either of them as they are friends. Little crush number two…hmm…let's just say I think I am crushing on how he has allowed me to enjoy myself this summer and the fact that I have spent most of the summer days at least spending some time of the day hanging out with him and a group of other people. Yeah…people have been asking if something is going on, but definitely not…he's just one of those guys you can't help but love to talk to.

◆ ◆ ◆

It may have been more than two weeks late, but I started my period today…well somewhat if you consider one measly drop of oddly colored blood for the entire day a period.

This afternoon while Hayley was babysitting, I went to the park to run. It was somewhat therapeutic running through the woods...yet somehow a relief considering my binge on brownies and chips yesterday. I kept the calories down to a minimum of 300 today until dinner at Olive Garden with my mom, brother and Hayley. I chose one of the lowest calorie meal choices containing only 250 for the lunch portion. I also ate three bread sticks and some salad which brought my total calories for the day a little above what I planned, but oh well.

◆ ◆ ◆

It seems like so much has happened in the last week. I suppose that's because it has. I got caught in a lie the other day. It's pathetic that of all things I could lie about, the one that I get caught in and in trouble for is about food. Yes, food. I lied about food. Hayley was over and asked if I had already eaten today. I told her and my mom that I had made a peanut butter sandwich. They didn't believe me despite my efforts to convince them. My mom opened the dishwasher to find the knife for evidence. I wasn't worried. I figured there would be a knife in the dishwasher used for peanut butter sometime earlier. Hmm...imagine my surprise when she could not find one single knife in the dirty dishes and then their surprise when they realized I had lied. My mom even looked at me and started crying. I hate having to lie to them about what I eat. I always tell them I eat more than I do and now they won't ever believe my word.

◆ ◆ ◆

    Chris stopped by the other day when Steve was over. Steve wasn't in the room and out of the middle of nowhere Chris popped the question that was hot a few months ago. I just wasn't expecting it from him and especially at this time. It really caught me off guard. He asked me if I had an eating disorder. I didn't know exactly how to respond. I couldn't find the words to answer it. Luckily I didn't really have to. He said he heard that I did from a few different people. Months ago I would have wanted to know every detail about who told him and what they told him but I have learned to not worry about other people but to focus on changing my habits for myself.

◆ ◆ ◆

    Yeah so crush number two…well, if it's at all possible I believe something may have happened. Let's just say the last few days have been strange. I feel almost as if I play some deranged character on some comedy style soap opera. How the incident began and why, I wish I knew. One minute I am playing super tennis on Nintendo and the next minute he is on top of me and we are making out on my den floor. Later that night while looking through old family albums, it happens again. He started kissing me. The next day…the same thing. And the day after that was not much different either. Yeah so it started with us hanging out every day which lead to occasional flirting but making out was not intended. At first it was kind of exciting but that quickly changed. One night after he left all I could think about was how badly I wanted to talk to Rory. I felt guilty about kissing him and realized it didn't feel right. I didn't get the same feeling I used to with Rory and I don't want to be "that kind of girl." Yeah, he is a great guy and I love hanging out with him but I know I just want to be friends.

◆   ◆   ◆

So, I called Rory. Just talking to him made me realize how much I still love him. He agreed to get together the next day so we could talk. Overall I think it was the best thing I could have done. I needed to see him again, I needed to make things right, or to at least have the satisfaction of knowing I tried. It wasn't easy, in fact I cried quite a bit. The reason I cried so much was because I realized how badly I had hurt him and how I made a huge mistake. Just being in his arms is one of the best feelings. Even after two months those feelings have remained. Some feelings I didn't even realize were as strong as they are until I saw him again. He's still not ready to be friends. I hurt him badly. It is difficult for him to understand what I was going through at the time and why I seemed to take everything out on him. Hopefully soon he will come around. I really miss having him in my life.

Now I wonder what I was thinking. I can't place feelings where they don't belong. "He" came over tonight. All I could think about was Rory. When he tried to kiss me goodbye, I quickly turned my head and gave him a hug instead. I think that was one of the best decisions I have made recently.

◆   ◆   ◆

A flood of negative thoughts have been racing through my mind. I need to start writing more and think less. It seems like I live through so many emotions in one day that it becomes difficult to skip days of writing. Everything builds up inside me like a time bomb waiting to *explode. The explosions are what I am afraid of. I am afraid that one day I will completely freak out and fall back into my past eating habits. The other day I just broke down and started crying. I miss the way my thighs didn't touch at all, the thinness in my face and how skinny my arms were. I miss the way my hip bones stuck out. I was looking at pictures from spring break and I desperately want to look that way again. What was so wrong with the way I looked? Yes I know it wasn't healthy but was it really that bad? Of course it was bad and I can't let myself think I want to look like that again. I need to let it go. Let go of my obsession with calories and the weight I have gained. Please help me let go.*

◆ ◆ ◆

Today I had my first day of volunteering at Hospice. I can tell that this is going to be a wonderful experience. I am even looking forward to volunteering again next week. There was only one moment I spent thinking about my weight and that is because of what I found in the storage room. While Hayley and I were retrieving the water cart, I noticed a scale lying smack in front of the door. I spotted it right away and I couldn't stop staring at it. I was mesmerized by it. Right in front of me lay the truth. How much bigger I had become in the last two months. I was so tempted to go back and discover what these past few months have done to me. I am so afraid of stepping on a scale again because I fear that the number will only contribute to a damaging fall. As much as I am drawn to it the more repulsive it makes me feel.

◆ ◆ ◆

The other night I got really drunk. I know I shouldn't have let myself absorb all of those calories so I ate very little yesterday and went running today at the park. I also lied…again. I have been lying every day to the people I care most about. The worst thing is that I am not doing it intentionally to hurt them but it keeps falling right back in my face, making me look even worse. The lies I tell are meaningless. For example, Hayley asked the other day if I had eaten dinner. I told her I ate a turkey sandwich. She knows I lied about it. It has become almost compulsive, I always tell her I eat more than I have. The only reason I lie is because it's hard to have them breathing down my neck making sure I eat. Hayley knows me all too well though. I knew we were going to be drinking that night so I chose to limit my calories during the day.

◆ ◆ ◆

Last night I ended up sharing parts of my eating disorder and self image problems with Katie. One of the guys we were with walked up to her and pinched her side commenting on how she shouldn't be eating the pop tart in her hand. He wasn't serious, of course, considering Katie is beautiful, but being the jerk that he is I can see how it came across that way. Apparently Katie is self conscious and this comment only made things that night worse. She was upset and came to the conclusion that she was fat, ugly, and was not going to eat anymore. She was bawling and just wanted to be left alone. It hurt me so bad to see her thinking so negatively and not seeing who she really is. She wouldn't listen to anyone's comforting comments so I decided to explain what I had been going through. As much as I dislike talking about it, I felt that someone else could actually benefit from my mistakes and it was important to share my story.

◆ ◆ ◆

I came up with an interesting idea today. Sometimes when I am bored, I feel that I need to be munching on something or eating to keep me calm and happy. Well today I decided that I am going to start chewing gum more frequently. It seems like the perfect solution. Chewing on gum will help stop me from stuffing my mouth with calories I do not need. This just might work...at least I hope so.

◆ ◆ ◆

Part of my struggle is plain and simple. Part of me doesn't want to eat right. In fact, I miss some of my old habits. Yeah so maybe everything I felt and went through at the time was hell. But to be honest, parts of me want to give up and slide back into the gaping pile of shit that became my life. It just seemed easier. I eat because I know I am supposed to and I want to be healthy again, but eating makes me feel guilty. Every time I eat I become disgusted with myself and the excess skin I can pinch off my body. I just want it to all go away.

◆ ◆ ◆

The little things upset me. Comments that no one would think twice about provoke a negative connotation in my mind. At breakfast with my family I ordered strawberry pancakes with whipped topping. It was a very generous portion yet I easily managed to finish them off. As the waitress took the plate from the table she commented "Wow, you must have been hungry." Maybe to most people that comment wouldn't have meant anything, but to me what she really meant was, "you fat bitch, you really did not need to eat all of that." Her remark was no different to me then when I am munching on some snacks and my mom says, "wow, you must really be hungry." To me it does not matter how they meant it, because I just look at the comments as a way for them to remind me that I am nowhere near a perfect body shape.

♦ ♦ ♦

I am so frustrated. As much as I want to get over Rory, I don't want to even more. I don't want to forget about him. I want to always remember everything we shared. I don't want things to change, yet at the same time I want everything to change.

♦ ♦ ♦

My medication causes me to have some strangely bizarre dreams. Last night, I had what I would consider to be my worst nightmare. I actually woke up scared. The fact that the dream scared me as much as it did, is disturbing to me. It was about gaining weight. I dreamed I had stepped upon a scale only to discover I weighed nearly 118 pounds. I woke up literally sweating and feeling hot and flushed all over. Thank God it was only a dream. Before I started down this path to an eating disorder, I weighed 118 pounds. Although my goal is to gain weight now, I don't want to weigh that much ever again.

♦ ♦ ♦

Yeah, so I ended up seeing Rory tonight. It was a fortunate accident, considering he is still not ready to speak to me. I was at a friend's house in Bowling Green (BG) and had no knowledge of the possibility *of him showing up. Apparently he did not know that I would be there either. He barely even looked at me. It was ridiculous. I grabbed his hand and dragged him up the stairs so I could talk to him. I told him that he could at least try to be friendly when we run into each other somewhere. We talked about everything once again. I understand that he needs time before we can be friends again. I just hope that the time comes sooner than later. I don't want him to vanish out of my life forever.*

◆ ◆ ◆

I ran into Rory's mom today at the library. I haven't seen her since we broke up and our conversation was more than pleasant. After talking to her, I feel great. I told her a lot of information that she did not previously know. While talking to her, all I wanted to do was cry. In fact tears did form in my eyes. When I think about it, I think the whole situation would be easier if he was completely in the wrong. Such as if he cheated on me. But knowing that I am the cause for our distance right now is even worse. If this eating disorder had not developed, everything could be different. But it did and I cannot forgive myself for that. If it wasn't for the evil voices in my head I wouldn't have taken everything out on him and consistently carry a stormy cloud over his head and mine. If only I had realized how wonderfully he treated me. If only I knew better than to toy with his emotions. If only. That is all I can imagine right now...those what if's. Right now I don't care what it takes. I want him to know how much he means to me. Yes, I will give him space, in fact I truly believe that is the best thing I can do right now. There's a quote that fits my feelings perfectly. "Just because I have moved on, doesn't mean I have given up." Maybe I will move on, and in some ways I think I already have, but I won't give up on him. I will always be there whether he asks for me or not. No one can ever take away what Rory and I shared together. Perhaps that is what really matters.

◆ ◆ ◆

Today I hopped on the scale while volunteering at Hospice. I couldn't resist. The temptation was stronger than I had anticipated. I wish I hadn't stepped on the scale. I wish I could have retrieved the water cart from the utility room without giving in. I wasn't pleased with my current weight. I can't deny that I knew I wouldn't be pleased before I saw the weight I have gained. Because of that, I went running tonight. I am going to say this hoping it will be the last time I will have to…FUCK SCALES! There is no reason I should become short of breath before stepping on one, fearing the number that appears. Honestly who cares about how much I weigh, besides me? For now on when I run it will be for the mere purpose of staying healthy and in shape, not to please a scale.

◆ ◆ ◆

Aside from the whole weighing myself on the scale incident, today turned out to be a very uplifting day at Hospice. I learned the true meaning and power behind the words "Til death do us part" while witnessing a male patient and his wife. His wife sits with him hours upon hours daily and quietly waits while he sleeps. While delivering fresh water this afternoon I overheard her softly whisper, "I wish there was a guest room upstairs so I could stay here every second with you." We talked to another patient today who greatly appreciates life. She kept repeating that you are only young once, while discussing relationships, *and spring break. While discussing Rory she used one of my mom's favorite, yet annoying expressions "there are many fish in the sea." I couldn't believe how much she was willing to share during our first visit with her. They live their lives learning more lessons than I can even imagine. They have seen things and felt things I won't be able to experience for years to come. Despite their current situations, they are so fortunate and appreciative of everything they have been given.*

◆ ◆ ◆

Right now I want nothing more than to be in Rory's arms. The thought of his presence soothes even the deepest of cuts. I don't want him to listen, to give advice, or compliments. What I want is simply the touch of his arms around my shoulders and a sincere hug. To feel the power of his words through silence. The comfort of his eyes telling me that everything is going to be okay. Now after my emotional breakdown over a simple "misunderstanding" of my mother's choice of words, the one thing I crave is the one thing that I lost.

◆ ◆ ◆

I can't help it. I don't know why I take everything the wrong way. I came home from Cedar Point this evening and had previously eaten a sub from Subway. When I walked in the door, my mom asked me if I wanted some freshly cooked salmon (my favorite) and rice. I told her that I already ate. I realized she went out of her way to make it just for me, but I knew in my mind it would lead to more calories than I cared to consume. Ten minutes later I went to reach on top of the refrigerator for a handful of fat-free pretzels, while she cut in with "I thought you already ate." At that moment I felt disgusted and all I wanted to do was hang my head over the toilet and go for a long run. I interpreted her response as "why are you eating junk food? It will make you fat." Why do I allow myself to think this way?

◆ ◆ ◆

I successfully downed a hamburger from Wendy's along with a small fry last night for the first time since I can even remember. I didn't realize until then how amazing fast food can actually taste. Of course had I not been drunk, maybe I would have enjoyed the taste even more. Then again I'm sure I would not have let my friends coax me into eating so much grease and fat. I absolutely despise the fact that I have eaten so much unhealthy food lately.

◆ ◆ ◆

I haven't written in the longest time. So much has happened in the past few weeks that it seems as if every emotion I have ever endured is strung together in a never-ending web. My feelings are so varied. Depending on the day, one minute I can be an emotional wreck yet the next I question whether or not I really care about what bothered me so much the day before.

◆ ◆ ◆

Right now I don't believe I could be more disappointed with myself. I ate a small amount of food today and I was proud of it until 20 minutes ago when I got home and downed balls of cookie dough, along with half a bagel. I have heard that anorexics can move from one extreme to the next. I will not allow myself to move to the extreme of binge eating. For nearly a week I have been telling myself that I need to start eating the way I was six months ago. I promise myself every night before I go to bed that I will start my old habits again the next day. Unfortunately either my fabulous plans are ruined due to an impromptu dinner out with my friends or I simply give into my hunger pains. Ok I know this is wrong. I can't let myself fall into those habits again but I would like to restrict my eating once again to some extent. Anorexia controlled my life once. I trust that I have the courage and wisdom to stop it from getting out of control again. Although I look back at that Alyssa with disgust and hate, I admit that in some ways I am starting to miss her more and more. I miss the power. I miss the "high" I felt knowing that I could deny myself fattening foods. Maybe I couldn't control school, my relationships or the future, but at least I had the satisfaction of controlling something. Anorexia was both the enemy and friend. Sometimes I felt like it was all I had. Maybe that is why I am starting to crave it again and that truly scares me. I continue reminding myself that I lost so much to it and was close to being left with nothing. Remembering those months brings back numerous bad memories that I never want to live through again. Every time I think about the way I felt emotionally, I want nothing more than to curl up in a corner and cry. I hate thinking that so many other girls have or are dealing with that weight on their shoulders…most of them probably alone. I wish everything about this eating disorder could just end, but I fear that in many ways it never will.

◆ ◆ ◆

Rory is finally talking to me! We have even gotten together a few times in the last few weeks. We went to dinner last night and then hung out at my house for a few hours. Things are still somewhat weird between us. I know that both of us are still hurt from the past but I'm hoping we can manage at least being friends. We know each other in ways that no one else does. Just spending an hour or two with him a week is perfect. There are no attachments and neither of us intend to rebuild a serious relationship which is relieving. For once I feel like I can just take things as they flow. Of course right now it's difficult to refer to him as just my "friend." Maybe that is because recently we have engaged in somewhat intimate situations. But honestly, I'm not complaining.

My Unstated Sin

Strong on the shell
yet weak underneath
smiling through the day
but at night I do weep
pushing fears aside
striving to hide
the pain held within
an unstated sin.
-Alyssa-

◆ ◆ ◆

The other night my friends commented on a picture taken out by my pool early this summer. I hadn't seen the picture until then. My friends kept discussing how disgustingly thin I looked and how the bones in my ribs stuck out like knives. Katie even went so far to say that I resembled a Jewish Holocaust survivor. What relevance considering Hayley had used the comparison months before. As much as I hate when *my friends comment on how gross I looked or look, I love to soak it up. Aside from their comments being annoying, I am given a sense of satisfaction. I crave being thin, possibly more than I crave food. The hardest thing in recovering has been finding a healthy middle ground.*

◆ ◆ ◆

One of my strongest attributes has always been honesty. Dishonest people have been my biggest pet peeves. However, over the last year, I feel that I no longer have the right to judge others by their circulating lies and disloyal friendship. For if I choose to turn my back on them, I have also turned my back on myself. The past half year has been filled with lies told to the ones who care most about me. The ones that have lived these times with me and stood by me with patience. Although they were small white lies, they reflected the big picture. A picture that I tried to hide. After months of counseling and support, I am still lying. "I'm not hungry," "I'm full," "I already ate," "No, I don't like that." The lies have become second nature. My mind no longer has to think. In a sense, I think I have begun to believe the lies I tell. My mind now controls my body. I have told myself so many times that I'm not hungry that my body actually feels full.

◆ ◆ ◆

While playing a game with my friends or eating at a restaurant she catches me and nods her head in disgust. I do it so subtly I barely even notice. I grab the skin on my sides, arms and thighs and try to look down on my body as others see me. When I notice her glaring at me, I quickly cover up by profusely scratching the area. But I know it is too late. Once again, I am caught. Fortunately, no one else seems to notice the hourly pinch test I perform on my body in search of excess fat. Or at least they don't give me blank stares or comment. I look down to erase the thoughts in my mind as I feel guilty and childish. When will this fully escape my mind?

◆   ◆   ◆

Ten minutes before heading to Ashland to visit family, I broke down. Why? I wish I knew the answer. It was a two-hour drive and I refused to eat before we left. My parents knew that if didn't eat beforehand, I would not eat the rest of the day. I bawled while my mom shoved spoonfuls of applesauce and a half cup of yogurt down my throat. I screamed and hollered as they yelled back, "Don't embarrass us this weekend Alyssa. You need to eat in front of all the relatives." It's frustrating knowing that my grandpa's eyes will be watching me constantly. I won't feel comfortable sitting down at the table to eat or even going to the restroom. I feel like I will be judged. This is pathetic. My parents even threatened that I will not be able to attend OU next fall because it is four hours away and they are afraid I will not be able to take care of myself. Little do they know that this threat doesn't phase me. I know their comment was made out of frustration. Can't they see that I'm just as frustrated with myself?

◆   ◆   ◆

I've noticed that in common situations I may never feel comfortable again. I get flustered and my heart pounds in discussions about anything weight related. One of my friends while flipping through a yearbook noticed that someone a few grades lower had gained weight over the summer. She was extremely thin the year before. Her bones *stuck out and her skin was pale. Without hesitation someone blurted out "wasn't she anorexic?" It amazes me how everyone at my school seems to be obsessed with weight gain and loss in fellow classmates. The major topic of conversation at lunch centers around who may be anorexic, bulimic or a binge eater. It is disgusting to hear others poke fun of what I know as a very serious and dangerous disorder.*

◆ ◆ ◆

Anorexics seem to not only be preoccupied with what goes in their mouth, but in everyone else's as well. I seem to have urges to go out of my way to see what other people eat. I think that's where the frustration began to kick in. If I saw what I considered an overweight person eating pretzels or pop tarts or cookies I immediately figured I couldn't eat it or I would become fat too. However, I would watch my friends and other thin girls eating cookies at lunch along with fries and couldn't understand it. They were thin! You would think after witnessing that I would allow myself to indulge like they did, but that wasn't the case. One by one I slowly labeled my favorite foods as forbidden. Quickly confusion and irritability set in. Why could they eat whatever they wanted and look great when I couldn't? Well it took a long time and I am still struggling with the answer to a long waited question. I can. If only I had realized that before the problem slowly escalated out of my reach.

Hope

Hurtful cries
and sobbing tears
all built up from a never-ending year
of whispers in the halls

> *and check up calls*
> *a long road of curves*
> *with anxious nerves*
> *trying so hard to win the fight*
> *perhaps one day I'll see the light.*
> **-Alyssa-**

♦ ♦ ♦

While at the mall with my mom today, we stopped for lunch at Ruby Tuesdays. I originally ordered a grilled chicken wrap with mashed potatoes, until I noticed they offered an alternative menu indicating the calorie content of their entree's and sides. I then discovered that by changing my order to a turkey and lettuce wrap and coleslaw I would cut my calorie intake in half. As soon as our waiter came by, I informed him of my change in order. I think I fell in love with Ruby Tuesdays today.

I was dedicated. Dangerously dedicated to losing weight. In fact, on evenings I had to babysit, I did not even think about letting that come in between my exercise routine. As soon as I put the children to bed, I spent the remainder of the evening doing crunches, jumping jacks and running in place. Approximately 15 minutes before their mother was expected to be home, I stopped to cool down and wash the sweat off my face.

◆ ◆ ◆

As I grabbed my change from the self check out, it explodes out on the front cover of the notorious "Star" magazine, "Who got skinny, Who got fat?" What happened to who the hell cares? Despite my utter disgust, it's gossip that interests me and I am ashamed to admit that. Why media cares so much I will never understand, but I do understand that I also need to work on not caring.

◆ ◆ ◆

Tonight I met my family for dinner at Chili's. I drove separate planning on heading across the street to run to the dollar store and Target to pick up some gag gifts for my friend's 18th birthday. My mom while eating, expressed her interest in coming along with me. I wanted her to come, but at the same time I had other plans. Plans I could not inform her of. I tried coaxing her into meeting me at Target after I ran by The Dollar Tree but she insisted on coming with me at that moment. I thought my idea for the past week had gone down the drain. I had previously seen a bottle of metabolism enhancing pills intended for weight loss at The Dollar Tree. (Yeah, The Dollar Tree, I'm sure those work). Of course however, I am willing to try anything that will boost my chances of losing weight, although unpractical at times. I grabbed my findings at the dollar store that I intended on purchasing and headed to the check out. On the way, I grabbed the pills and placed them underneath a bag of Skittles. I felt my heart racing as I kept my eyes on my mom who was walking around aimlessly wasting time. Finally, my turn. As the employee placed the items in the bag and I walked out the door, I felt so relieved. I had pulled it off and my mom had no idea.

Little did she know, I had also found a bottle of One a Day Weight Loss vitamins at home that I had been taking every morning for the past ten days. I knew it wouldn't be long before she noticed, so that is why my idea of the metabolism pills came to mind. At Target I asked my mom about weight loss vitamins and dietary supplements, feeling guilty the entire time. On the way home, following moments of silence with the exception of the drowning sounds of Keith Urban on the radio, I burst. "I bought diet pills at The Dollar Tree." Those eight words were spit out so quickly, it's amazing she actually caught them. Her reaction was not what I had expected. Based on her and my dad's reactions lately to my recurring habits, I expected anger. Instead, after brief silence she responded quietly with "give them to me as soon as we get home." For the remainder of the ride we did not speak, although I could hear her softly crying. Once we pulled in the driveway, she thanked me for being honest. Later on, I opened the medicine cabinet. She did not waste any time. The One a Day Weight Loss Supplements were gone.

◆ ◆ ◆

Every fiber supplement, including mineral oil has been taken out of its usual location. I suspect my mom knew that I occasionally turned to them. In a time-consuming attempt to find them, I succeeded. They were located in the back of my mom's closet on the top shelf inside a basket with other weight loss vitamins and fiber supplements.

◆ ◆ ◆

Skimming the cover of a magazine, it pops out, "How to shed weight fast" and "How to get the body you desire." Quickly I rummage through the pages hoping that perhaps this article will shed a new light in my goal to achieve utmost perfection. I grab the magazine from the stand to read while my mom checks out in line. I skip past the pages dealing with current events and celebrity scandals to dive right into the issues with losing weight, including the new gossip on the recovery of Mary Kate Olsen. I soak up as much information as possible while my mom signs the receipt. I walk away reflecting on the new tidbit of information I discover.

◆ ◆ ◆

This morning on a bus ride for a school field trip I overheard a phrase far too common, "I could never be anorexic because I love food too much." I laughed to myself, specifically recalling a time that same sentence left my mouth a year ago. The funny thing is, anorexics love food too. In fact, they do in most cases even more. I think that explains why eating disorders are such a battle. It's never easy to struggle with something you love.

Things I have learned:

-While beginning recovery **no one** will say what you want to hear, either way you're not satisfied.

-Not eating and running will make you extremely light headed and fatigued.

-Eating then exercising excessively afterwards will make you sick.

-In your own eyes, you're never satisfied with your body.

-Constant exercise, little food and winter = being miserably cold…all the time.

-The people you thought would never annoy you, will.

-Lack of fat in foods you consume=lack of boobs.

-No matter what you think your family and friends do care.

-No anorexic has one mind. You have two. One that knows what's right and one that does not care. The first step is acknowledging this.

-Get rid of scales. They are your competitors. You compete against them daily pushing for a lower number, but you realize, you will never win.

-Don't think your counselor is working against you and won't believe what you say. Most likely if she doesn't believe you, it's because your lying to your self.

-It's a harsh reality, but some classmates will look at your problem as a huge joke and will poke fun. Forget them. They are not worth your tears.

-It's okay to not know what the future will bring. It's also okay to be scared.

-People will say things that will hurt you. You will be in situations in which you feel uncomfortable, and it is unavoidable.

-When you lie to others, you are only lying to yourself.

◆ ◆ ◆

I keep walking back and forth. I'm panicked, anxious and afraid. I haven't felt this bad in a while. The thought of throwing up right now feels reassuring. I feel fat. No one is home. What's stopping me? The pain. The damage. I walk in the bathroom, flip on the light, walk back out turning it off. I sit down and turn on the t.v. burning through the channels. I start running. I stop. I am still considering making myself throw up. "Let it go," I tell myself. I don't want to make myself throw up. I look through the medicine cabinets searching for some sort of laxative or vomit inducer. No luck. I keep searching until I find mineral oil. I settle. I still feel terrible. I can't throw up. I won't. The urge is strong, yet unsatisfying. I'm not giving in.

◆ ◆ ◆

As I slipped on my tennis shoes this evening, my parents immediately objected. I told them it would be a short run but their reasoning was based around my low fat dinner and three-set tennis match earlier today. There was no sense arguing. I knew they would not cave in, so I pretended not to care. After I thought their attention was focused on reading the newspaper and discussing their day, I made my move. I went upstairs to my room, turned on the radio and started running in place. Ten minutes later my door swings open. I quickly stopped and pretended to just be stretching, but they knew better. I can't hide anything from them anymore. My constant urge to exercise is driving them crazy. Geez! Just leave me alone! My evening workout was over for now, but I won't stop trying. Later, I tried sneaking to the basement, but as soon as they heard the door open, I was quickly stopped.

◆ ◆ ◆

I miss how the top of my thighs did not touch. I miss the satisfaction of pushing them together in an effort to push myself harder. I miss the way my ribs popped out minimizing the fat on my body.

◆ ◆ ◆

The leaves have begun to change color and fall from the branches leaving them bare. I glance upwards picturing the bark as my former self. Bare, cold, lonely, dull and lacking body. I love the color of the leaves in autumn. The bright red, oranges and yellows as they sway back and forth. It's after they fall condescendingly, that I am haunted of the past, and left fearing the coming winter months. A breeze of cold air, sends endless shivers down my spine reminding me of the chilling effect last winter left. Everything I experienced last winter, I want to forget, but I can't. I feel as if I will be dreading not only this coming winter, but every winter that follows. Afraid of slipping into a white blanket of frost, or haunted by the ghosts of that year and the painful memories.

◆ ◆ ◆

Sometimes, I wonder why I even bother going out of my way for other people. If I knew my deeds were appreciated, it would be well worth it. But I have helped some people and have been there for them in ways I know they would never return. Even people that contributed in making situations in high school unbearable at times. I did what I thought was right. I look at some of them now, disgusted. It's true...a thank you does go a long way. I just wish some people knew how to say it.

◆ ◆ ◆

My heart starts fluttering and I cannot stand still. When anorexia or the topic of weight is brought up, I panic. The word anorexia sends shivers down my spine. I feel so uncomfortable. Today, while in the line at lunch, two of my table mates stood behind me while the one commented about how two other girls in our lunch, do everything together because as she put it "they share a special anorexic bond." The sarcasm and humor in her comment, is what pissed me off. Later that day, in newspaper class, I discovered that not only is one of the features going to be about prescription anti-depressants, but also anorexia and bulimia. Yay, I can't wait to read the article on that…Perhaps someone should write about how people that do not understand eating disorders should learn to shut their mouths.

◆ ◆ ◆

I have already started to find myself beginning to dread lunch. Last year, lunch was hell for me. I always wanted to skip it, to avoid the comments made by the group I sat with. I begged my mom to schedule doctor appointments around those times. If I could change that year, I would have gone and sat in a teacher's room during lunch instead. Today I did just that. The first half of the day had been a long one and I knew if I went to lunch, it would only seem longer.

◆ ◆ ◆

I followed through with the senior PHS tradition of wearing a sports bra to the big rival football game. I was hesitant; not because of the 40-degree weather, but because I lack confidence in myself. When it comes to my body, I am conservative. In the summer, I hate walking around in a swimsuit even in my own backyard. I hate feeling judged.

◆ ◆ ◆

Caught in lies again. Today I was told by Hayley that she no longer trusts me. She asked me this afternoon what I ate for lunch at school. I told her I had yogurt and a turkey wrap from the sub line at school. "No, you didn't. All you had was yogurt and a bite of a cookie, I asked Christina today what you had for lunch." Oh great, here it comes, I thought to myself. The fact that my mom was in the room did not help. I got bombarded with questions as to why I am still lying. To be honest, I do not even know why I still am. It is compulsive. My mom is tired of my lies. She had been taking my word only to find out my word cannot be trusted. She now plans on monitoring my meals more closely again and requesting print-outs from my school of my purchases at lunch.

◆ ◆ ◆

I can feel myself slowly slipping. This past week I packed a tight lunch consisting of mostly carrots and rice cakes, or a 50 calorie cup of pineapple applesauce. I have been keeping a close count of calories consumed. I have even resorted to working out and running in my room every night again. My dad came in the other night begging me to stop. His words, "You're not doing this again Alyssa, I let you get away with working out last night," rang like an alarm through my ears. I am scared. I have been doing a great job eating better, but I worry that my mind is taking over trying to confuse right from wrong. I know what I am doing, I won't allow myself to stop eating but the thoughts are scaring me. My mom asked me today if I needed to schedule a visit with

Barbara again. She caught on over the last week to my over exercising habits and negativity towards my weight and body again. I told her I did not think I was at that point and she said she trusts that I know when bad habits are resurfacing.

◆   ◆   ◆

This morning at breakfast with my family, my dad started talking about my tennis awards banquet the other night. He told me he was proud of me for receiving the awards I won, but told me he was most proud when he watched me get up and grab a piece of pizza to eat, since he could not remember the last time I was able to do so, without being told.

◆   ◆   ◆

I do not know what it is, but I can feel the chill of winter already stinging my body and mind. The wind and early darkness is an instant reminder to the pain I suffered beginning last winter. I feel as though there are ghosts of the past haunting me. Yet the ghosts are my own. The voices in my mind, the weakness in my legs, the pounding of my heart. I fear the ghosts will never go away, however it seems as if they shall only appear during the cold winter months and slowly tiptoe away as sunshine resumes. I fear the cold, the darkness, the palpable inner monster that this town possesses during this season. I need to get out. I cannot wait to leave next fall for college although I shall only be a few hours south. Perrysburg is a great place; a great place to grow up and raise a family, yet I need to get away. I want to move to where winter is more bearable, for a chance to rid of these demons so that I can leave them behind once and for all.

"Every now and then I catch myself slipping into the same old thoughts, but this time I am strong enough to catch myself before I actually fall."

About Rory...

I get off the phone and sigh as I sprawl out on my bed. It's one of those nights. The nights I miss him. I miss talking to him. His voice being the last I hear before I sink into a deep slumber. I smile. It's almost as if I feel him lying next to me. I remember the way his arms wrapped around me and the way my hand fell perfectly into his.

It's not supposed to be this way. Six months after our breakup and for the most part, nothing has changed. Not one day has gone by without him popping into my mind. I often catch myself replaying moments from the past. He remains not only in my heart, but in my mind. Some days I think about him a lot, other days he runs by for merely a second. Still, every day. I would have thought that after six months things would get easier. That I would get used to him not being in my life like before. That I would be getting over him and become interested in new relationships. I have gotten used to the change. The only exception is if it is at all possible, I miss him even more. Some days I almost catch myself about to call him to share exciting news, or exchange a quick I love you. Then I stop myself and remember. I remember that those days are the past. A past that I need to let go of.

I have spent the last few months being busy and productive. Trying to get to know new people, and just focusing on building confidence in myself. I spent the summer trying to shift my feelings for Rory to other people. I don't want a serious relationship, however I have agreed to not shut out new people without giving them a chance.

Dave, who I met through Brett, came to visit this weekend. I have been talking to Dave frequently and he is someone that I know would be a good friend. While Dave was over, we watched old family videos. One was titled "Christmas 2003" and I could not recall what was on it. I popped it into the VCR. Up pops Rory, with a familiar sounding "Merry Christmas." Well that's an interesting start to the night…Dave meets the infamous Rory.

I kissed Dave, yet made sure nothing was taken past that. I enjoyed kissing him as I had developed an infatuation for him over our late night conversations on the phone. Despite the crush, when I kissed him, I still thought of Rory. Our phone calls continued until I realized I couldn't use Dave as a band-aid for my heart.

◆ ◆ ◆

Last night while in Columbus supporting my tennis team in the state tournament, I met up with Rory. I was really excited to see him, because it had been nearly two months. After seeing him, I feel much better. Right away, he commented on how good I looked, and he continued throughout the night telling me I looked great and much better than in the summer. I needed that. He has no idea, how much that meant to me. I felt good about myself, and even proud.

◆ ◆ ◆

It's that time of year again-about a year since this whole ordeal and my obsession with losing weight began. The cold weather musters up memories I'd rather forget. I will probably always associate the cold weather, bare trees, and gray sky with the emptiness I felt this time last year. Every now and then I catch myself slipping into the same old thoughts, but this time I am strong enough to catch myself before I actually fall.

November, 2004

Rory and I are talking regularly. He came home the beginning of November and we spent some time together. We were also together over Thanksgiving. Our times together lately resemble the way things used to be before all this craziness of my eating disorder took over. He will be home for about a month in December for Christmas break. I am not sure where things are headed, but I am certainly happy to have him back in my life if only as a friend. I am definitely happier overall than I have been in a long time. Looking back, I know we needed to be apart in order for me to help myself.

"Only time will tell."

The Aftermath

Do I want to forget it? Yes. Will I allow myself? No. I still think about it a lot. I think about slipping again, decreasing my food intake, and increasing the daily exercise routine, but I won't. Those are the moments I have to pick myself back up. I guess the question I think all anorexics wish they had the answer to is; Can I recover? Honestly, I don't know how to answer that. I know I have improved mentally, and without a doubt, physically as well. However, everything about this disorder is not gone. I still worry about my weight. I still suffer remembering the past year, and I know I will always continue my obsession with calorie content. I believe recovery is more than possible. I do not, however, know whether to believe a total recovery is possible. Only time will tell.

Anorexia is becoming far too common in young women and men. During my high school years, there was a lot of teasing and poking fun of individuals who had lost or gained weight. Although many teens go through temporary phases of diet and exercise, others head down a long, dark path to destruction often alone. Sadly, as I write this book, a member of our junior varsity tennis team entered a treatment facility for an eating disorder. It is my hope others will begin to realize that a person suffering from an eating disorder needs the emotional support of friends and that immature and mindless comments only make the situation worse. Physical appearance alone does not define an eating disorder. Just because a person is thin does not mean they should be classified as anorexic. Anorexia is much more than a physical disease. It is emotional as well. People suffering from anorexia vary in size and many anorexics are thin from the onset of the disorder. One does not have to be extremely underweight to be in danger.

In the midst of putting this book together I have been forced to relive painful memories. In some ways, it has been very therapeutic. It has also been hell. As I recalled each memory, I felt a sense a relief almost as if a heavy chain was slowly lifted off my back.

As difficult as this past year has been, I consider myself lucky. Lucky to be walking down the path of recovery and lucky for the opportunity to share my story with others.

I will forever be grateful for the family and friends who stood by me when I needed them most. I reached rock bottom once and I will fight as hard as I can to never see it again.

Ending Comments

Janet Biederman

After reading Alyssa's heart-wrenching journal, I knew she had the ability to reach out and help others by sharing her story. For me, her journal is a reminder of the hidden pain and memories of a past I hope we will never be forced to relive. For others, I believe her journal will provide the peace and hope necessary for healing by realizing they are not alone in their struggles. I have never been more proud of my daughter than I am right now. She is an amazingly beautiful young woman who has fought hard to find herself and realize what an incredible person she is both inside and out. We launched a battle and I am happy to say we are winning!

0-595-34147-0